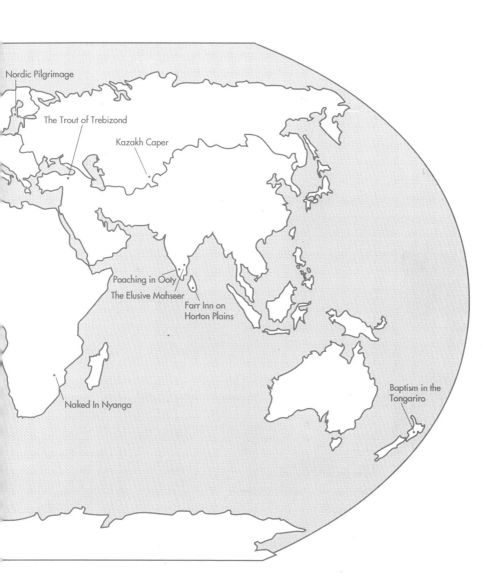

Nordic Pilgrimage

The Trout of Trebizond

Kazakh Caper

Poaching in Ooty
The Elusive Mahseer
Farr Inn on
Horton Plains

Naked In Nyanga

Baptism in the
Tongariro

The Revenge
OF THE
Fishgod

To Michael,

Best wishes for your retirement.
Hope to see you in India one day.
Tight lines,

Kevin and Christine
Andrews

1999

The Revenge
OF THE
Fishgod

ANGLING ADVENTURES
AROUND THE WORLD

Carl von Essen

Introduction by William C. Black

Illustrations by Neila von Essen
Maps by Marianne von Essen

PAUL S. ERIKSSON, *PUBLISHER*
FOREST DALE, VERMONT

10 9 8 7 6 5 4 3 2 1

Library of Congress Cataloging-in-Publication Data
von Essen, Carl, 1926-
    The revenge of the fishgod : angling adventures around the world / by Carl von Essen ; introduction by William C. Black ; illustrations by Neila von Essen ; maps by Marianne von Essen.
    p.   cm.
    ISBN 0-8397-7115-0
    1. Fishing—Anecdotes. 2. von Essen, Carl 1926- —Journeys.
I. Title.
SH441.V66   1996
799.1'092—dc20   96-22403
                               CIP

For Kerstin

Acknowledgments

I AM DEEPLY GRATEFUL to my wife, Manisha, for the inspiration and the encouragement to write about what I love to do. Bill Black of Albuquerque has been a constant source of support and friendly criticism. Also Steve Bodio and Phil Muilenburg gave me much help in learning about writing. Thanks, all. Special appreciation goes to my daughter, Neila von Essen, for her evocative drawings and to my cousin in Sweden, Marianne von Essen, for the maps. Lee Berman solved the dark mysteries of programming and electronically transmitting these words from muse to publisher. Peggy and Paul Eriksson have given me invaluable editorial advice and support.

Trachinus draco, the Fishgod's messenger, shown on the cover and in several other locations, was drawn by Ingrid Benson.

An angler is always learning. I thank my fellow members of the Anglers' Club of Wrentham, Massachusetts, for their patient efforts in teaching me more about fly-fishing and fly-tying, both of which have increased my affection for this gentle and contemplative sport.

Introduction

PUBLISHERS TYPICALLY CATALOG their offerings under headings such as "fiction," "poetry," "cooking," "how to," and so on. Very few books fail to fit into this scheme. Remarkably, Dr. von Essen's *The Revenge of the Fishgod* defies classification. This is the essence of its charm. Imagine a literary recipe blended by a naturalist, world traveller, philosopher, gourmet—and angler, flavored with a series of accounts of encounters with fish of many sorts, sizes, and dispositions, and all cast in diverse geographic settings and circumstances. As such, the fish provide a necessary matrix, yet there is no attempt to teach us how to catch them. Rather we are encouraged to savor the totality of an angling adventure, the geology of the place, its people and customs, the flora and fauna—and to take some quiet time to reflect upon our private selves. As I have, you'll find Carl von Essen to be a most delightful companion as you accompany him around the globe from the land of the Vikings to the slopes of Patagonian volcanoes—and points between.

William C. Black, M.D.

Contents

MAPS

RECIPES

Preface

THE FISHGOD PROTECTS THE HONOR OF ALL FISH. At least that is my belief. What happened one cold and rainy day on the Kattegat made me a believer.

I never suspected that the following infractions were on his list, a.) fishing as an adult with a worm, b.) shooting fish with a rifle, and c.) using tackle with a breaking strength greater than the weight of the fish.

These and other transgressions against his kingdom led to consequences that I will relate. Perhaps the reader can take warning and avoid the fates that befell me.

But read no further if you expect to experience vicariously the dramatic capture of the prey after a suitably extended foreplay of the stalk and the strike.

I hope the unexpected happening, the failure to hook, or the loss of the quarry evokes a sympathetic resonance ("yes, that could have been me").

Much of my story has little to do with fishing. I often escaped my medical duties to see the countryside and meet its people. And I enjoy eating (note the meaning of the German verb *essen*), and fish recipes are scattered throughout this book. Yes, I believe the Fishgod acknowledges that fish are hunted and eaten. But he insists upon a culinary preparation worthy of the victim.

I am sure he approves highly of fly-fishing, the gentlemanly way, to which I am a convert, albeit rather late and inconstant. And, of course, he must applaud the latter-day ethic of catch-and-release, taken up with tremendous zeal by American fly-fishermen and now spreading around the world. I practise it also but confess to keeping selected fish for epicurean adventures.

As a scientist, I cannot avoid giving an occasional taxonomic description, or some interesting biological and ecological morsel that may be digestible.

Why fish with an angle for sport? Because we remain atavistically hunters. The predatory instinct strikes a deep and resonant chord in the male psyche. Some of us hunt to remain sane in a topsy-turvy, mechanized, frantic world. Manisha, my psychologist wife, is bemused but tolerant. But the most lethal weapon I have used, with one exception, is a fishing rod.

Angling is, however, a special branch of the chase. Isaak Walton added the subtitle, *The Contemplative Man's Recreation*, to his classic *The Compleat Angler*. That opportunity for contemplation has great meaning for me. What is it, 'to be at one with nature'? It is a rare experience. But when it comes, it is immediately and powerfully recognized.

Why then write about it? Because these experiences deserve conscious expression (and also catharsis). And that expression pays homage to our natural environment, which is slipping away from us at a remarkable rate.

Others have done far better at this. I believe one of the greatest among modern angling writers was Dana Lamb. In *Where the Pools are Bright and Deep,* an example of his prose as poetry is shown in some sentences set up as verse:

> The springtime mountain air was sweet;
> The sun was shy behind the clouds;
> The swallows had at last come back
> To pluck emerging mayflies from the surface of the stream;
> The robins caroled from the lilacs on the village lawns.
> (Winchester Press, 1973)

Need much more be said?

The Revenge

OF THE

Fishgod

Prologue

I<small>T WAS A COMFORTING MEDIUM</small> that enveloped me with soft sounds and flashing lights of many colors. I heard a distant constant chord of music, as if from the voices of angels. I did not feel my body; I floated like a spirit through that universe; I was a *délok* for a moment—the Tibetan who departs his body and then can return.

I was drowning.

An enthusiastic cast with the fishing rod had toppled this eight-year-old boy overboard and no one saw it happen. I do not know how long I was in that watery world but my next memory is that of Father's startled face as he revived me. The rest is hazy, but I later learned that I had held the rod firmly throughout.

To this day, some sixty years later, the recollection of the experience is vivid and somehow agreeable.

So ended the first day in my life of fishing. That was my first brush with the Fishgod and his minions. But not the last.

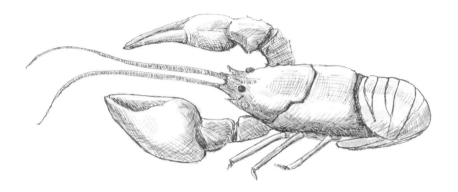

CHAPTER 1

A Fish That Is Not a Fish

This has nothing to do with fishing, at least the type with rod and reel. But the finding and trapping of crustaceans fulfills a hunting and foraging instinct shared by many peoples around the world. The subsequent gustatory rituals are often remarkably similar. For example, the devouring of the Atlantic lobster may be attended with brightly decorated bibs, funny hats, and napkins and is often festively enhanced by lubrication with champagne. The bright-red, hard to catch, and expensive invertebrate with an exoskeleton somehow supplies the excuse for celebration. And the Scandinavians are no slouches at celebrating. In addition to describing the crawfish, I digress to another Nordic feast involving rotted herring. And I include a bit of creative chemistry in concocting akvavit, the water of life, essential to most Nordic feasts.

DEEP-ROOTED IN THE NORDIC PSYCHE is a tradition and primitive ritual that involves this fish that is not a fish. The freshwater crustacean *Astacus fluviatilis* (the river craw- or crayfish, crawdad) is associated with my childhood images, as from a Bergman film, of midnight fishing adventures, of joyous feasts, song, and endless speeches.

Astacus and its cousins live in the temperate regions of both hemispheres. The crawfish are closely related to lobsters that inhabit the salt seas. The crawfish-to-be emerged millions of years ago to inhabit freshwater lakes and streams. The north American and European crawfish, in fact, is a nearly exact, but smaller image of the north Atlantic lobster.

One Tasmanian variety may weigh up to nine pounds; most others are a good deal smaller. They are scavengers but also feed on smaller aquatic animals.

In the Mississippi Valley crawfish feed on rice during the night. This infuriates the local farmers who regard them as pests. There is a limerick that begins, "Ten thousand Swedes marched through the weeds. . . ." If those Swedes were sent down to the Mississippi paddy fields with nets and traps, the crawfish problem would be quickly solved to everyone's gustatory satisfaction.

The crawfish grows by periodic moulting of its shell. It mates in the late autumn. The eggs are attached to the under surface of the tail where they are fertilized and remain until hatching in the spring. The best time to gather crawfish for the pot is in late summer, before the breeding season.

For centuries the European crawfish has been enjoyed for its delicate taste. There have been many ways of preparing it; for me, the one and only way is the Scandinavian.

But first, the essential prelude and part of the ritual of eating it is catching it. My memories are of tribal fishing expeditions that were great adventures for a small boy.

My father, then stationed in San Francisco, was among the earliest Scandinavians in the 1920's to recognize the similarity of the West Coast crawfish to its Nordic cousin. In those days crawfish were largely untouched by the Americans, and only a few enterprising

Frenchmen, Italians, and Scandinavians sought them in the coastal streams and lakes. Being largely ignored by Man, the Pacific Coast crawfish were often huge, approaching the size of lobsters. They had few natural predators beyond infancy, when they were prime fare for steelhead and otters.

The traditional season for the annual ritual was August.

The adults had then moulted, leaving them with fairly soft shells, thus permitting an easier dissection of the delicate morsels in various body parts.

The usual scenario occurred on weekends. The more adventurous Swedes would assemble on Saturday afternoon, well equipped with traps, gunny sacks, and scraps of slightly rotten meat, and a large holding tank that my father had built. The expedition went by auto convoy to, in those days, the Russian River, some sixty-five miles north of San Francisco. The rendezvous was at the North Beach ferry terminal for the forty-five-minute ride to Sausalito (yes, the Golden Gate Bridge construction had just begun in 1933). At the river they hired rowboats and canoes for the night and established a command post on the sandy shore. They baited and set out traps about dusk, and started a roaring campfire. At about hourly intervals, the men would check the traps, and empty, rebait, and move them if the yield was low. They roasted sausages and devoured them along with liberal helpings of potato salad, beer, whiskey and coffee. For me the memorable part was toasting marshmallows.

But accompanying the men out in the boats at night was a small boy's heaven. The dark, smoothly flowing water reflected the flames of the distant campfire. The fishermen raised the traps, lighting up their contents with flashlights. The startled crawfish flapped their tails and raised their large claws at the intruders. It took a certain skill, and, yes, bravery, to handle these aggressive crustaceans. After a few unforgettable gnashes I learned the timing and dexterity needed to pick up the furious prey. Into the holding tank went hundreds of crawfish. Finally when enough had been caught, usually after midnight, the crawfish were transferred to wet gunny sacks and the expedition returned home.

At home, we emptied the gunny sacks into our bathtub, which was filled with continuously running water. All of us slept soundly and long after such an outing.

The next day, the preparation for the evening ritual began. My mother filled a huge vat of salted water, brought it to a boil, and added bunches of fresh dill crowns. Then my father and I gathered the crawfish in batches of twenty or so, carefully and humanely immersed them tail first in the vigorously boiling water, then removed and replaced the now brilliant red and correctly cooked creatures at ten minute intervals.

They were then cooled and eventually chilled in the refrigerator along with large quantities of beer and akvavit. Loaves of San Francisco's own sourdough bread were made ready for heating in the oven. The festive banquet table was set with paper table cloths and napkins having bright red crawfish designs. Chinese lanterns were mounted overhead.

Why Chinese lanterns for an atavistic Nordic rite? Perhaps it arose in the eighteenth century when our King, Gustav III, brought continental manners and fashions to Sweden. It was just then when European courts admired and borrowed much from the newly appreciated Chinese art and culture.

The tables were set, candles lighted and the guests arrived. Let the games begin!

Swedes are great believers in rituals and ceremonies. They seem necessary in order to open up the shy spirit of this introverted tribe. The story goes about two Norwegians, two Danes and two Swedes marooned on a deserted island. Many years later they are discovered. The rescuers find that the two Norwegians had been continuously fighting each other, the two Danes had learned to brew beer and had opened a restaurant, and the two Swedes had never spoken to each other—because they had never been introduced!

Various feasting rituals have helped to overcome that problem. Besides the more or less Christian feast days of Christmas and Easter there are several more primitive events.

Walpurgis Night involves bonfires, singing, and carousing; Ålagille, the Feast of Eels, includes the attempt by blindfolded guests to catch a live, slithering eel in a barrel of water.

But the August crawfish feast is the most universally enjoyed. The dignified persona is dropped with a thud, and a more natural, open, and—yes—garrulous Swede emerges.

It is not just the alcohol, it is the ambiance and tradition. It is hard to remain dignified when sucking, chewing and otherwise devouring piles of lobster-red crustaceans, washing all down with akvavit and beer. "Skål" rings out and a long series of drinking songs begins.

The traditional toast, "Skål!"(or "skoal"), also means "bowl." It derives from "skalle" meaning skull. The connection is said to be this: the early Scandinavians drank toasts from the sawed-off calvariums of their vanquished enemies.

The Viking banquets in Valhalla must have resembled a crawfish party. But unlike the revelers at the feasting-hall in Asgård, I have never seen a fight nor heard an unkind word at a crawfish party.

The technique of eating crawfish varies from person to person. Some are selective, delicately picking out the meat from the claws and the tail, even removing the "vein," the large intestine. The "butter" is a white fatty substance under the carapace and is admired by all.

The other school devours everything possible, leaving only a pile of calcareous shells on the plate. Yes, I mean everything. There are in the gastrointestinal system of crawfish, like other crustaceans, nameless greenish and brownish organs and structures containing unmentionable products of their scavenging appetite. It is all fair game for the crawfish gourmand. Just close your eyes and devour. It is actually delicious. I can attest, from years of experience, to eventually eliminating all compunctions of delicacy.

The little boy sat with the grownups at these feasts and took in everything. He especially admired the long, humorous, witty, and wise speeches that gave another dimension to the primitive rite.

My father had a role in preserving that rite in his homeland. Beginning in the 1940's a fungal infestation began to decimate Scandinavian crawfish populations. Swedish fisheries experts sought to control the epidemic, without success. They sought a solution by searching for a strain of fungus-resistant crawfish. They eventually evaluated the Pacific Coast species.

A team of experts came out to San Francisco and were greeted by consular officials. Father was considered the local expert and brought them to our country place in Marin County. There, on Papermill Creek which flows into Tomales Bay, they caught their first California crawfish, literally in our backyard. These and other samples were sent back to Sweden for testing. They were found to be fungus-resistant but otherwise essentially identical to the Swedish species. An official decision was made to repopulate the entire infested Swedish-crawfish waters with this species.

A brood stock was fished from Lake Tahoe, 2000 feet high in the Sierra Nevada. These crawfish were considered the least likely to carry contaminating organisms. They proliferated readily in Swedish waters.

Nowadays the majority of crawfish caught in Sweden originate from Lake Tahoe. They are called "*signalkräftor*," i.e., signal crawfish, after a distinctive small white patch at the base of each claw. From either snobbery or very acute taste buds the native crawfish is more prized than the California species and is slightly more expensive, that is about three dollars each for four-inch crustaceans. No longer are they the giants that we fished in the old days. With a consumption of fifteen to twenty crawfish for each guest at a posh Swedish party, the cost for the host is considerable.

Since those early days I have introduced my non-Scandinavian friends to this delightful tradition with unanimously enthusiastic responses.

Although the preparation sounds simple, even the cooking of crawfish has a certain ritual which should be carefully followed.

TO COOK CRAWFISH

10-20 crawfish per person

1½ to 2 Tbsp. of salt per quart of water

Fresh dill crowns (the seeds should be yellowing for
 the best and strongest flavor)

Optional; 1 Tbsp.of honey and 1 slice of yellow onion
 per quart

The water should be more than enough to cover the crawfish. The crawfish are ideally kept in clean running cold water for 12 to 24 hours to clear the gastrointestinal tract (especially for gourmands like myself). Get the water to a rolling boil, add the salt, honey and onion, and half the dill. Cook a reasonable number of crawfish at a time, keeping a rolling boil. Add the rest of the dill. Cover and cook 10 minutes exactly. If time permits, cool the crawfish in the stock, but eventually chill them in a refrigerator. Finally drain and arrange on a platter decorated with more fresh dill.

Serve with quantities of heated fresh or sourdough bread and butter. Freezer-cold akvavit is mandatory. I prefer the lighter and sharper taste of Aalborg (Danish) or Skåne (Swedish) brands. Never drink akvavit on an empty stomach and do not sip it. Quantities of beer should be available. Alcohol-free beer or mineral water will allow a longer distance with the akvavit.

A word about *akvavit*. *Aqua vitae*, the Scandinavian water-of-life, appeared in Sweden sometime during the fifteenth century when some ingenious souls discovered the potent properties of the distillate from fermented grains and potatoes. Abuses naturally followed and by the end of that century, Sten Sture, Guardian of the Realm, passed a law outlawing the distilling and selling of *akvavit* in Stockholm. But its history has had ups as well as downs. In the sixteenth century a plague epidemic forced the Crown to seek all possible remedies. One included a unique *akvavit* concocted by the court physicians. It contained the powders from unicorn horn (actually narwhal tusk), red coral, ivory, and deer antlers as well as a variety of herbs and spices. No data is available concerning the effectiveness of this mixture.

Healthy mortals today, however, can create for themselves far more palatable concoctions from a few basic ingredients—and more cheaply than by buying some of the brands of *akvavit*. Start first with the best brand of vodka such as Absolut. Then let the imagination run wild. The traditional ingredients that give *akvavit* its refreshing bite include fennel, caraway, anise, and dill seeds. Start with a mixture of a teaspoon or so, add the vodka, say a cupful, and let steep for a month at room temperature in a tightly sealed bottle. Then taste it, decant or filter, and dilute it with enough vodka so that the herb flavor is subtle, not overpowering. Then chill and serve. A dash of sherry or Madeira mellows the flavor and can produce a concoction similar to the famous Danish Aalborg *Jubileumsakvavit* or Norwegian *Linieakvavit*, which travels back and forth across the equator mellowing in old sherry barrels as ballast on Norwegian freighters.

But numerous other ingredients can be used as well. Consider berries, such as raspberries or blackberries, or ginger, cinnamon, cardamom, coriander, saffron, lemon or orange peel, and even chili peppers. There are scarcely any limits to taste.

A parallel seasonal rite in Sweden is feasting on rotten herring—yes, rotten. Let me explain about *surströmming*.

Freshly caught small Baltic herring are placed in saturated brine for one day, then gutted and decapitated, washed and salted down in large barrels. They are allowed to stay in the warmth of the Scandinavian summer for six or seven weeks. A distinct and overpowering aroma of rotting fish results.

When the process is judged to have reached the correct degree of putrescence the herring are canned in large oval tins. The process of bacterial fermentation continues and the tins may swell and distort to alarming proportions because of the formation of malodorous gases.

The cans are cautiously opened in the outside air, allowing the rank smell to dissipate. The herring are served directly with sliced onions, bread and butter, and, as usual, with plenty of *akvavit* and beer. The taste is unique, a dramatic flavor of fish that is without parallel.

Enthusiasts for *surströmming* can be fanatical, swearing by one brand or another. They look down with disdain upon the faint-hearted who loathe the dish. The cult worshipping *surströmming* reminds me of the afficionados for the tropical fruit, the durian, with its abominable smell and its supposedly divine taste.

To my knowledge no cases of fatal or even of slight poisoning have occurred. Yet the very process reminds me of the conditions under which botulism occurs, the consequence of the toxins from *Clostridium botulinis*, an anaerobic bacillus, closely related to *Clostridium welchii*, which causes gas gangrene. Somehow the processing of *surströmming* avoids a fatal or even unpleasant outcome.

Thus each culture has developed over the centuries certain tastes that relate to the available ingredients and to the practical methods of preserving or preparing them. And, if they are seasonal, a bit of ritual enhances the enjoyment. Many of these tastes may not be universal, rather acquired and cultural, perhaps even archetypal. The enjoyment of *surströmming* certainly could be such a taste.

But the setting adds to the experience. Recently my wife and I stayed in a cabin by a stream in Finland. We gathered mushrooms and lingonberries. We cooked the crawfish given to us by neighbors. While they cooled, we heated ourselves (in a sauna) to a bright crawfish hue, then cooled by plunging into the river. When both the crawfish and we were sufficiently cool we sat down to a memorable meal, framed by the silent forest and waters of the North.

The forest trolls must have watched us with approval.

CHAPTER 2

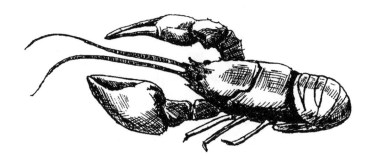

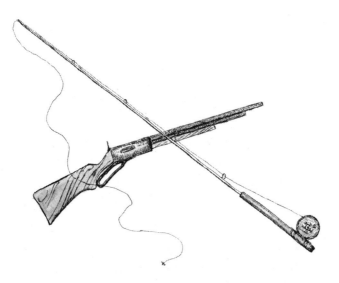

No Bears in Trinity

The year was 1944. We were students at UC Berkeley and deferred from military service for premedical studies or flat feet or other Selective Service exemptions. The curriculum was on a wartime schedule—no summer holidays. We were burned out from the intensive program, and a week between semesters was an enticement to get away. It was time for a drastic break from the mind-numbing studies. Why not a hunting trip? The fact that none of us had the foggiest idea of how to hunt was no barrier. We certainly didn't know it would turn into a fishing trip—of sorts.

WE LEFT BERKELEY LATE FRIDAY AND DROVE ALL NIGHT. The three of us had spelled each other at the wheel through the long journey from Berkeley. Driving through them in the darkness, Redding, Whiskeytown, and French Gulch seemed like ghost towns. Weaverville glowed pink as dawn glimmered to our right and the old Buick began to climb the foothills of California's Trinity Alps. Only an hour more until we reached our goal, a hunting lodge in the Trinity Primitive Area.

We were literally armed for bear and anything else. I had a rented .30/30 caliber Winchester, Bruce backed up with his .22 caliber automatic, and Bob was our guide.

Bob had served in the CCC, the Civilian Conservation Corps of Roosevelt's New Deal era. He did his service in the Trinity Alps and described in glowing terms the abundant game of this last vestige of primeval California. He promised that deer and bear were to be seen in every direction.

But Trinity was 300 miles north of Berkeley. Wartime gasoline rationing was strict. Our friend Ron lent us his car but no gasoline. Bob had the gasoline since he worked nights in a garage. Bruce and I provided the artillery. We had sleeping bags and some scanty camping gear. Bob knew old man Carr, an eccentric Trinity character, from CCC days, and had arranged for us to stay in his lodge in Carrville, founded by his pioneer forebears and located at the tail end of the dirt road going into the Trinity wilderness.

When we finally rolled into Carrville, consisting of one house and a barn, we were dismayed to find the "hunting lodge" locked and deserted. Communications had gone awry. We were now dozens of miles away from civilization, food, and lodging. What to do? To turn back would consume our gasoline reserve for the return trip.

We had come this far, three tyros armed to the teeth.

"What do we do now?" I asked.

"Let's camp and start to hunt. Maybe the old man will be back in a day or two," said Bruce.

"I know where we can start. There's a good campsite a mile beyond the roadhead," said Bob.

We pushed on, assembled our gear, and hiked up a small valley, led by our intrepid guide. To our great surprise no deer bounded across the trail nor bear showed a face. After several hours of reconnoitering, all that appeared were our ravenous appetites. Presently, to our great joy, we discovered an abandoned orchard which provided an abundance of apples and blackberries. We set up camp and had a sumptuous feast of bread, sardines, apples, blackberries, and water. We placed our sleeping bags around the bonfire and slept soundly that night.

In the morning Bruce broke out a large container of pancake flour for our breakfast. But then I heard him cry, "Oh no, It's full of weevils!"

Perhaps mistakenly we discarded the contents into the fire. Weevils, after all, are an excellent source of protein. We were left with remnants of bread plus water for sustenance. Only Tug, Bruce's cocker spaniel, was well supplied—with canned dog food. We carefully checked the labels only to find, to our disappointment, the warning, "not for human consumption."

We were, truly, innocents adrift, a trio with naïve pretentions of surviving in the wilderness. Our stomachs were now achingly empty. In a determined effort to find nourishment I explored the banks of a small creek. In the depths of a pool I spotted numerous small trout. How to catch them? Luckily I had brought along a small metal telescopic rod and reel with line and hooks. No flies: those were the dark ages of my fishing experience, very dark indeed. . . .

All of us turned to a concerted worm hunt. With sticks, utensils, and fingers, we foraged through the damp soil and retrieved a number of wriggly creatures destined for ultimate sacrifice.

Given this ammunition I found a strategic position at the head of the pool, having just enough sense to conceal myself from the quarry. The baits were floated into the depths of the pool with rewarding results. Over the next half-hour we harvested a mess of six-to seven-inch rainbows, sufficient to provide a temporary stop to our path toward starvation. Those rainbows, it turned out, were really steelhead smolts. The sacrilege of devouring babies that could someday be noble twenty-pound fighters would be exceeded only by a deed that I must now gradually unfold. And all this, I feel certain, was duly noted and recorded by the Fishgod.

Our expedition gained new strength and determination from its sumptuous breakfast of trout and bread. We set out again to find our elusive quarry. Nothing. Time passed and spirits sank. All thoughts were again focussed on food. The beautiful, then pristine wilderness of the Trinity Alps was all but ignored. Since entering the region we had not seen a soul. The quest continued.

Suddenly a covey of small California quail strutted across the path in front of us. Silently Bruce unlimbered the .22 and let loose with a fusillade. The birds vanished in a cloud of dust, but distressed sounds indicated that damage had been done. Now it was Tug's turn to demonstrate his qualities and importance to the expedition. The cocker bounded into the bushes and retrieved three quail that provided us with yet another Spartan meal.

The next day, when we reached the upper stretches of the north fork of the Trinity River, an astonishing and unforgettable sight greeted us. As far as eye could see, thousands of large fish were moving upstream. Often half out of the water, they skidded and wriggled up the shallow riffles to the next pool, rested, then pushed on.

Such a big spawning run of, as it turned out, coho or silver salmon is now a past memory in the Trinity, and, indeed, most coastal streams of the lower forty-eight. Either the waters are dammed or polluted, or the spawning beds have been largely destroyed.

After a moment of admiration of this spectacle demonstrating once again the power of sex, we felt our predatory instincts, triggered by empty stomachs, assert themselves.

"All we need is one of them," said Bruce. "Yes, but how can we do it?" asked Bob. We had no nets, the fish were too fast and slippery to catch (we were not bears), and the tiny rod and line were useless against these large fish.

We looked at each other. Then, with a single thought, we looked down at my deer rifle. I voiced the thought of us all; "Let's shoot one."

The Fishgod muttered a malediction, and countless anglers of history, from Isaak Walton to G.E.M. Skues, rolled in their graves. We three neophytes were oblivious.

We planned the attack: Bob was stationed at the tail end of a riffle, Bruce was the spotter, and I was the hit man. We clambered up a steep bank overlooking a shallow pool where the salmon were relatively quiescent, thus affording a clear shot. We somehow guessed that concussion, not penetration, was all that would be needed to stun the fish, which would then be retrieved by Bob.

The river valley echoed with the sharp, loud reports of the .30/30. One may ask: where were the fish and game wardens? There were none. This was wartime and the countryside was deserted. The laws broken during this expedition were never counted.

Aiming at a salmon's head, I succeeded in stunning a large one, which turned belly-up and floated downstream only to be missed by Bob. After a while we became better coordinated and a second fish was dispatched and retrieved. It was a twenty-five-pound silver sided coho, sufficient for our ravenous appetites.

We cleaned the fish, wrapped it in paper, and drove to the lodge. Still, no one was there. Considering all the alternatives, we decided to break in, occupy the place, and cook our catch. Bob assured us that old man Carr could not be far away and would not mind our action. In fact, we discovered that the rear door was unlocked and so we quickly took over the place. In a cooling room were large pans of fresh milk set out for cream separation. With milk, cream, butter, potatoes, and other vegetables from the garden, and the salmon, we had the first truly satisfying feast of the trip.

We turned in for a good night's sleep in sleeping bags on real beds and awoke the next morning to the sounds of an arriving car.

It was our supposed host, exceedingly drunk. In fact, we never saw him sober. No, he did not mind our trespassing; yes, he knew we were coming but made some vague excuse about visiting his daughter, more likely so he could booze it up in Weaverville. His arrival marked the transition from a period of exciting, albeit illegal, adventures to a time of relative comfort and luxury. We abandoned pretensions of hunting wild game. The beauty of the surrounding forests, mountains, and streams was, for the first time, absorbed into our youthful psyches.

Three rested and happy students returned to Berkeley with renewed zeal for the heavy work schedules. We shot no bear. What would we have done with it?

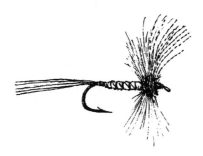

CHAPTER 3

George and the Hammonasset

In the 1960's we lived near New Haven in a bedroom community close to North Branford. The scene resembled that in the novel and film, Peyton Place. *The following two stories merely scratch the surface of those goings-on. I was, generally, more interested in the fishing.*

THE HAMMONASSET FLOWS DOWN TO LONG ISLAND SOUND just west of the Connecticut River. Now, thanks to dams and the thirst for suburban development, it is a pale shadow of the once respectable small New England river that supported the spawning of native sea-run brook trout, salmon, shad, herring, alewives, and eels.

When I was introduced to the Hammonasset thirty five years ago by my neighbor and friend-to-be, George, it was still a sturdy stream, but the brookies had been essentially replaced by stocked brown trout. Some became anadromous natives that migrated each fall from the salt water to spawn high up on the shallow gravel beds. There were rare sea-run brookies.

George, like all true fishermen, was a solitary angler and only reluctantly, after much coaxing, brought me along one dark dawn to his secret stretch of stream. His was a deadly technique—upstream worming. I was eclectic in those days, with only the bare rudiments of what fly fishing later came to mean to me. I was impressed to watch a real hunter stalk his underwater prey and began to learn the same technique.

That part of the Hammonasset, close to the mouth, was not for fly fishing anyway—not unless one could cast an exceedingly tight and accurate loop of line through a veritable tunnel of vegetation overhanging the deep, dark stream. I tried downstream nymphing without success and gave it up to adopt George's methods.

With a short rod, small spinning reel, two-pound test monofilament, and a single night crawler draped on a longish hook, the art was to flick, even skip or skid, the bait a good distance upstream under the overhanging vegetation and let it drift back, bobbing along the bottom, with slack line and open bail.

His slow and stealthy approach was that of a stalking Indian hunter. George could thus arouse the attention of the most jaded and dour trout, often a lunker. The first sign would be a twitching of the line, which would cease, only to resume with a short run of line upstream, the angler, with adrenalin surging, properly forbearing to allow the slightest resistance. Finally it would happen—a long run stripped line off the spool. Then, and only then, would he close the bail and firmly strike.

The weight of the fish could be a shock. The subtle foreplay did not telegraph the dimensions of the quarry. The odds in his favor increased with weight. Any snag was a lifeline of salvation; the two-pound test line could not resist the force of a wise and heavy brown in the deep.

The stalking approach, as I learned from this master, came from very primitive instincts. The concentration focussed upon the prey was absolute—the Hunter's Trance. A half-hour could elapse without movement or any thought, only total absorption upon the slightest activity from underwater. The mind was remarkably cleared of extraneous cerebral noise—no brooding over domestic or professional problems, no plotting on besting a rival or winning a grant. The rampant male was in his element, the quest clean and primal. And also it was much cheaper than the cost of an expensive rifle and an African safari.

The exploration of the Hammonasset led gradually upstream to what George called, "Western-type water" and which I dubbed the "fly-fishing stretch." It became part of my beat while George generally stuck to his original stretch—which also happened to hold the larger trout.

George, a mechanic at Winchester's, was of Macedonian, not Greek, origin. A proud and sensitive man, he pointedly reminded me of the difference. Only gradually did he allow a friendship between us to develop. In spite of widely different backgrounds and occupations, our mutual love of fishing and drinking helped to cement a bond. I provided to the friendship a skill at the creation of an exemplary home-brew. My microbiology course at medical school had provided the basic concepts needed for good brewing. By using the best ingredients and avoiding the fatal effect of oxygen upon the fermenting wort, I brewed an outstanding and powerful ale which was regularly bottled for neighborhood consumption. Even the yeast was carefully selected; the American Type Culture Collection in Washington supplied the *Saccharomyces carlsbergensis* that was maintained through serial culture by a close friend in the microbiology department at Yale.

George took up the hobby, and I felt that our friendship had achieved an external symmetry—fishing and brewing. But fishing was the more serious and sacred rite, properly and regularly done on Sunday mornings. We left together from our homes, either in my Morgan two-seater or George's Chevy van. Those were wild times. More than once we left late Saturday night parties for an hour or so of sleep, and were on the road at four o'clock, three sheets to the wind, sobering up on coffee at the nearest roadside stand. We generally finished about ten in the morning with the five–fish limit (no catch-and-release in those days) and returned home to devour enormous breakfasts. Then, for me in the summers, came an afternoon of dinghy racing on the Sound.

I slept well in those days. There was an abundance of energy in our younger bodies.

To adapt to the varied conditions of the Hammonasset I had short, five-foot fiberglass fly rods and spinning rods made by the local tackle shop. My beat, the upper stretch of river, began with slow, meandering worming water that gradually changed to fly fishing riffles and pools. Carrying two outfits was a burden, but manageable with the help of a sort of back-sling for the spare rod.

Fishing began at first light. The stillness would surround me until I broke the mirrored surface of the stream. The trees dripped of dew, the distant rooster crowed, the worm probed the depths until it eventually connected with its dupe, an unwary trout.

As time passed I identified and memorized the holding spots. The upstream wading accelerated, and I fished a mile or more of stream in five hours or less.

I assembled the fly-rod where the stream opened into riffles, shallows, and pools. I was ignorant, then, of the sophistication of fly-fishing. No particular knowledge of entomology disturbed my random selection of the Coachman, the Adams, or the Hendrickson, fished dry if there were rises and wet if there were none.

One event, however, triggered the first clumsy efforts at fly-tying—the emergence of the green oak caterpillars. They fed on the young leaves in the spring and dropped by viscous threads slowly into the water from overhanging trees, arousing the trout to splashy rises. The action was highly selective, however, and I was forced to tie good imitations with green thread and yarn on correctly sized hooks.

I gradually came to appreciate the superior virtues of fly fishing; esthetic, creative, and not messy. It gradually captured my full attention, although I acknowledged, as I still do, that there is considerable art and skill in upstream worming.

For nearly ten years I waded and fished the Hammonasset and came to know, like a well-worn and comfortable chair, all its nooks and crannies. The river taught me much about fish and fishing, and about Nature. Its beauty, moods, and colors became etched deep inside and relived in my dreams, both waking and sleeping. At long, tedious, and boring meetings or conferences I would slip into the sweet comfort of daydreaming, very clearly, about one or another favorite spot on the river.

The seasons governed the moods of the river. My favorite was autumn. The brilliant hues of the changing leaves were reflected in quiet, cold pools. The air was crisp and occasionally a whiff of fermenting and rotting apples would drift from a nearby abandoned orchard. I will always associate that apple scent with the Hammonasset.

Autumn brought mushrooms and berries. I would clamber out of the river to gather *Russella*, *Agaricus*, *Lepiota*, or *Boletus*, and place them in the fishing creel. Wild grapes grew abundantly along the stream and their large leaves nestled and cooled the killed trout.

The culinary preparation of fish was my job in our household and I often experimented. Grape leaves have a subtle, sour taste which has been exploited by the Turks and Greeks in *Dolma* and other dishes. I figured that wrapping trout in grape leaves might add an interesting touch to the rather bland flavor of brown trout. I then added a stuffing of the wild mushrooms. The indigenous and delicious dish met the critical approval of family and friends.

HAMMONASSET STUFFED TROUT

PREPARATION

Trout, like all fish, must be as fresh as possible, carefully cleaned and gills and cardinal vein (the large vein anterior to the backbone) scraped out. If the trout is large, scale or scrape the skin and wipe the fish slime off with a cut fresh lemon. Finally, pat the fish dry. If it has been refrigerated, allow the flesh to come to room temperature. Do not remove the head, a valuable part of the fish, with delicate flesh in the buccal muscles (cheeks) and neck. To some, including Manisha, my Bengali wife, and to most Mediteranean peoples, the entire head is a delicacy worth savoring and chewing—to bare gristle.

INGREDIENTS

Fresh caught trout, salted and peppered throughout

**Wild grape leaves (canned Greek grape leaves in brine
  can be substituted)**

**Wild mushrooms (store–bought varieties can be
  substituted)**

Fresh lemon

A little fresh or powdered cayenne pepper

Butter and vegetable oil

Salt and fresh ground black pepper

RECIPE

Clean and dice the mushrooms. Sauté in fairly high heat with a little butter, oil, and cayenne pepper. Cook until fairly brown and dry. Cool. Stuff the trout bellies with the mushrooms, then wrap each trout from snout to tail in grape leaves, binding with string.

The cooking can be done in a variety of ways. If the fish are small, sauté them in butter and oil. If large, grill them slowly over charcoal, basting the grape leaves with oil and/or butter. Poaching can be done with a court bouillion of one fish-bouillion cube per liter of water, some celery, onion and carrot, and white wine. To serve, remove the grape leaves. They impart a subtle additional flavor to the delicacy of the fish.

Autumn also signalled the return of the sea-run browns to their spawning beds. The official season ended in mid-October in order to protect the spawning, but heavy fall rains would sometimes trigger their early return. These were big fish, as heavy as six or seven pounds. They could be spotted by their wakes in the shallow gravel stretches of the stream, preparing the spawning bed and ultimately depositing the roe and the milt. I generally contented myself to watch this stirring and primal ritual.

At other times, fishing farther downstream in the deeper pools, I did hook spawned out browns. They resembled salmon kelts, that is, lean fish with dark colored and battle- scarred skins.

During all those years I rarely saw another angler. The river traversed woods, meadows, and pasture. No human habitation or road was within sight except at the upper and lower ends of the two-mile-long beat. The seasons imprinted their changes upon the flowers, shrubs and trees so that nearly each visit would bring fresh revelations of color, texture, and patterns. In short, the river was a moving feast for the senses, delighting me with surprises.

Many years have now elapsed since our departure from Connecticut and other images have gradually taken the place of those from the Hammonasset, but these, too, are mostly scenes from favorite spots on rivers.

On a recent visit to Connecticut I made a pilgrimage to the Hammonasset. As so often happens when one revisits places of nostalgic memory, the experience was a disappointment. So it was with that part of the Hammonasset. Its banks were festooned with housing developments, its shoreline stripped of much of its former vegetation, and there flowed a trickle of water in the stream bed.

I beat a hasty retreat to my memories, which are immutable.

CHAPTER 4

The Ladies' Stretch

In Connecticut, our middle-class development was located in the forested countryside and included a communal lake which provided the seasonal recreations of ice-skating, bass and pickerel fishing, and swimming. The latter included midnight skinny-dipping. For me, a greater attribute was the proximity of a fishing stream.

THE BRANFORD RIVER IS SMALL, scarcely larger than a creek. Its course is only about ten miles from source to the outflow on the shore of Long Island Sound.

Like most New England coastal streams, it probably provided a spawning ground long ago for salmon and shad, but since colonial days a mill and the necessary mill wheel and millpond had halted the migration and put a stop to a valuable food supply for both Indians and settlers.

Instead, the Branford was now stocked with brown trout, of which some were lucky or smart enough not to be caught immediately. These survivors grew into lunkers that lurked in the dense forest of

29

underground snags and stumps. They were rarely seen, but experts like George, with the deadly upstream worm, could lure them and haul them up into the light of day.

Upstream, the Branford assumed the attractive character of a fly-fishing creek. There were riffles, shallows, and pools, even the occasional rapid. Unfortunately, for me, this desirable stretch of a mile or so was off limits. The State of Connecticut Fish and Game Division, through some mysterious act, had designated this, the best part of the Branford River, to be reserved for women anglers only. The "Ladies' Stretch," as George aptly put it, was within walking distance of our house. On weekends I would often take long walks and reconnoiter the stream, noting, wistfully, the trout rising all along its course.

I never saw a female angler. What a waste!

I brooded about it. I was not brave enough to consider out-and-out poaching, and there was the matter of conscience. This also ruled out bizarre schemes like becoming a transvestite.

One day an idea flashed in my head like the proverbial cartoonist's light bulb. Why not give angling lessons to my oldest daughter, then nine, on the Ladies' Stretch? She would hold the rod, I would guide her wrist, everything would be legal and everyone happy!

My daughter became an enthusiastic accomplice, though knowing full-well, at that early age, of my nefarious subterfuge.

We began with the upstream worm and graduated to the spinning lure. Many good messes of trout were brought back by my proud daughter. We then began fly-casting lessons. These were a bit difficult for a nine-year-old. I presently found myself, with a wary eye about me, "demonstrating" fly-casting. Of course, trout that happened to be in the vicinity of the fly often hooked themselves. I was forced to play and land them. There was, shame on me, no catch-and-release in those days. We enjoyed eating trout. Luckily, no fish warden was ever seen on the Ladies' Stretch.

My daughter enjoyed these adventures and developed into an enthusiastic fisherwoman and outdoorswoman. She has passed that enthusiasm down to her daughter.

It has given me singular pleasure to thread a worm onto my granddaughter's hook, just the same way that I did for my daughter those many years ago on the Ladies' Stretch.

CHAPTER 5

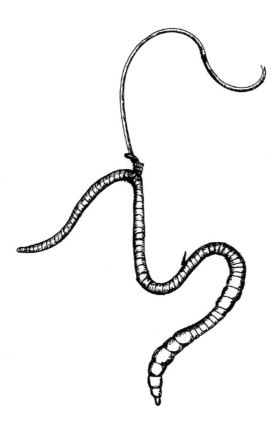

Piscatological Potpourri

I generally block out the numerous abortive, unfulfilled, or downright frustrating attempts to fish in various global corners. But quirky circumstances and peculiar people have often led to interesting, if not productive, angling experiences.

For example, in 1964 I embarked with my young family on what now strikes me as a foolhardy adventure—an automobile trip from Sweden to southern India, right through, although I did not know in advance, two wars and a cholera epidemic. We finished the trip, however, unscathed. This led to two angling episodes, "The Trout of Trebizond" and "Poaching in Ooty."

In 1972 I was invited to a scientific conference in Alma Ata, the capital of the then Kazakh Soviet Socialist Republic. I believe the deep suspicion by the Soviet bureaucracy that I was a spy resulted in my total failure to cast a fly in a fascinating and beautiful area of the world. This episode is titled "Kazakh Caper."

In 1980 my wife and I drove through northern Spain. In "Spanish Fly" I describe the attempt to fish the mountain streams of

the Cordillera Cantabrica near Reinoso which resulted in near ar-
rest for poaching on salmon redds of the Rio Besaya.

The Trout Of Trebizond

I N ISTANBUL I FOUND OUT THAT A CONVENIENT SHORTCUT to eastern Turkey was by packet ship across the Black Sea to Trabzon, the
modern Turkish name for Trebizond of antiquity. This would save
time as well as wear-and-tear on our new Peugeot station wagon and
on my infinitely patient first wife, Medha, and our three young children.

We had started from Sweden a few weeks earlier. The route was
through Germany, Switzerland, and Italy to Brindisi on the Italian
heel, then by ship to Patras in Greece, then through Turkey, Iran,
and Pakistan. My *"Carnet de Passage,"* issued by the Royal Automobile Club in London, was intently examined by the border guards.
They removed vouchers to document the transit of the car in and
out of Turkey and all subsequent countries. Failure to have this done
would have cost me the expensive bond left behind in London. Our
ultimate destination was Vellore, South India, where I was to spend
a year's sabbatical leave from Yale Medical School in order to set up
a cancer chemotherapy program at the internationally renowned
Christian Medical College Hospital, as well as to develop a clinical
trial for treatment of smallpox in Madras with a drug developed at
Yale. The idea of an automobile journey to India was enthusiasti-
cally endorsed by my family. But any convenient shortcut was welcome, and this direct and inexpensive sea route to Trabzon was
certainly that.

Early one morning we checked out of the rambling, dusty but
opulent Pera Palace Hotel and drove down to the waterfront. The

Bosporus was a cacophony of hoots, whistles, shrieks and bellows as watercraft of all sizes scurried in incessant, frantic but somehow orderly patterns. The centerpiece to the scene was the trim 3,000-ton packet steamer, "Trabzon," loading cargo, mail, and passengers. I drove the wagon down to an assigned spot on the quay. The family went on board as I anxiously watched the car, harnessed by nonchalant stevedores, lifted up by crane and swung on board. The procedure safely accomplished, we settled down for the two-day voyage along the Black Sea coast of Turkey, with stops at the ports of Sinop, Samsun, and finally Trabzon, the site of the classic novel by Rose Macaulay, *The Towers of Trebizond*.

Among the many passengers with whom we became acquainted was a young Turkish architect who was returning home to Trabzon for a family visit. He was fascinated by our planned adventure and invited us to stay with his family.

The entrance to Trabzon was not quite as romantic as that described in the novel. A coastal mountain range, the Anadoiu Dagiar, climbed up into the clouds. The town, no longer ornamented with its fabled towers, nestled around a tidy harbor, busy with traffic by fishing boats, ferries, and small craft. The Peugeot was safely deposited on the Asian shore and we drove a short distance to our host's home in the town center. His parents and wife were surprised but happy to receive us. Their house was a three-story dwelling facing inwards to a courtyard, reminiscent of older houses in northeastern Indian towns.

Although Turkey has been secularized since the days of Atatürk and both men and women wear western dress, old customs of Muslim heritage persist, especially, I am sure, in the more remote parts of Turkey. And so it happened with us, quite naturally, that the men and women divided into separate social spheres. My wife and two daughters stayed behind with the mother and daughter-in-law while I and our son went out on the town with the father and son.

We visited one café after another, sipping endless cups of tea (Turkish coffee is more common in eastern Turkey). We were, in a sense, being shown off to their community, but there was a genuine curiosity and friendliness. Communication was barely hampered by the language barrier. Inevitably, I came around to the subject of fishing and tried to describe trout and learn if they were found in this area.

There was a moment of blank stares before the father, his face lighting up, exclaimed, "Ah, *alabalik!*" Excited, he described where they were found in the rivers descending from the mountains behind us. I asked how they were caught and he described, quite vividly, an artificial fly. What luck! I had brought along a fly rod and reel but, alas, no fly line, leader, or flies. The father promised to supply me with the local terminal tackle with flies.

The next day he proudly presented me with the tackle: a heavy gut leader with a cast of half a dozen flies, all simply tied with white hen hackle. It all seemed a bit crude but I was not one to complain—perhaps the trout were huge and naïve.

During this time the women, including friends that had streamed in, had enjoyed each others' company, chatting, dancing, singing but also drinking countless cups of tea and eating delectable snacks. We all assembled together for the meals and I came to understand a little more about the sturdy, honest, and hardworking Anatolians—the descendents of Tamerlane—who, thanks to Atatürk, had escaped the deadening weight of Moslem orthodoxy.

Next morning we embarked on the long overland journey to India. The first leg was up and over the Anadoliu Dagiar range to the town of Erzurum. The dirt road followed the river Degirmen. This had been, I learned, until the building of the railroad from Erzurum to Ankara, the end of the long Silk Route from Central Asia. Thus, since the fourteenth century, Trebizond had steadily declined in importance. Once a major maritime trading port of the Genoese and the

Venetians, and even for a time a capital of Byzantium, it now was a sleepy Turkish provincial capital.

The first goal that day, however, was to fish for trout. The road steepened as we entered a gorge filled with pines and cypresses. The brawling stream flowed over and between boulders and deadfalls. It had all the characteristics of great trout water, and the water temperature of 55° at the elevation of 5,000 feet confirmed it. We drove up a side road to a likely-looking pool and I mounted the rod with the tackle given by my Trabzon host. Since I still lacked a fly-line I was forced to find a position upstream and to allow the tackle to stream down into the pool. I finally maneuvered the flies into a back-current that revealed some rises and—bang!—I had one on.

The fish burrowed deep into the pool and I struggled to keep it away from a tree stump that surely would have assured its escape. As I was playing the fish there came the sound of clattering hooves. I looked around, and there, bearing down on me as in the water well scene from "Lawrence of Arabia," was a turbaned horseman, complete with carabineer belt, rifle and sword. His approach was disconcerting and threatening and it was difficult to concentrate on landing the fish, which was a beautifully colored fourteen-inch brown. The fish was immediately released to my and the horseman's satisfaction. Then, in no uncertain terms, he indicated that we were trespassing on his territory. We had, in fact, encroached on tribal lands of the fierce mountain men of this spur of the Caucasus. So ended my limited foray into Caucasian fishing.

We drove on, through mountain snow storms, past Mount Ararat, and forded streams where bridges had been destroyed. We passed camel caravans, and transported Iranian soldiers and Kurdish tribesmen, cramming them into the back of the station wagon with our fascinated children. We passed numerous military checkpoints, were searched for weapons, drove across trackless desert, and finally reached the relative security of India. But all that is another story.

Poaching In Ooty

MAY IS GENERALLY THE HOTTEST IN INDIA. The monsoons break over much of the continent thereafter and a period of cooler, cloudy, and rainy, albeit humid weather follows. It was a good month to escape the one hundred twenty plus degrees in Vellore. We chose Ootacamund, "Snooty Ooty," the nearest high hill station, situated at an elevation of 7,000 feet in the Western Ghats (mountains) of southern India.

The route we took in the durable Peugeot was through Bangalore and Mysore City, then due south through the game sanctuaries of Mudamalai and Bandipur up to the cool and misty heights of the Nilgiris. Once settled down, I planned to explore the numerous streams that I learned had been stocked with trout since colonial times. But, again, I had no flyline except the remnants of gut leader from the Turkish episode. What could be substituted? I experimented with a variety of heavy cords and yarns. Those were the days after Indian Independence when the British had left in droves and the sources of supply for their sporting activities had virtually disappeared. Finally, I selected a heavy wool yarn, that, when wet, could cast a fly out twenty or so feet.

With this jerry built jury-rig I drove up into the hills searching for promising streams.

I was wading up one, casting futilely for non-existent trout, when an elderly Indian in a dhoti and tattered tweed jacket approached. Ganesan was the local fish warden and I did not have a permit. I was poaching. My excuse was that I had no inkling where to get one.

But he was forgiving. In broken Tamil and English we struck a deal—he would arrange to get the permit for me and lend me a proper English fly outfit if I would hire him as a guide. Done! The first guide I had ever hired—under some duress. I would not have escaped the poaching charge so easily elsewhere, especially Switzerland.

I picked him up early next morning. He had a beautifully pre-served Hardy cane rod and "Perfect" reel, complete with line, leader, and flies. It was a carefully cared-for gift from a grateful tea planter, re-turned years ago to his misty home in Scotland.

I was thrilled to have this turn of luck. We drove up to a forested valley with a gurgling stream that led to a pair of small lakes. I started fishing the lake which I found, in no uncertain terms, was a watering hole for the abundant game in the surrounding forests. The first en-counter was huge mounds of elephant turd, some fresh and steaming, others aged with an interesting variety of mushrooms emerging from the gigantic piles. There were *Lepiota*, *Laccaria*, and the universal meadow mushroom, *Agaricus*. I mused briefly upon the possibility of mushroom farming with this abundant source of compost. But then, in a moist stretch next to the lake, I saw the unmistakable pug-marks of a large cat. I called over Ganesan. "Yes, Sahib, that is pan-ther. Plenty animals drink here." He seemed unconcerned. My mushroom musings departed. Time for the business at hand.

There were no rises and no significant insect life at that time of day. Ganesan handed me a wet fly, a traditional British pattern called "Campbell's Fancy," and some advice on how to fish it. I cast it out with the beautiful Hardy rod and let the fly sink before slowly re-trieving. I cast again. There was a certain tingling on the back of my neck. Something, or someone, was behind me, watching. My casting was a little off. I kept looking back but nothing could be seen in the darkness of the nearby forest. I finally got the range, and one plump, beautifully colored twelve inch rainbow after another came to net. Ganesan cleaned them and we moved down to the stream. The fish-ing was good but anticlimactic. I was sure that somewhere behind, in the shelter of the forest, a panther lay watching me, bemused at the strange antics of a fly-fisherman.

Kazakh Caper

I N 1972, MY OLD FRIEND, LASZLO, A HUNGARIAN DOCTOR turned Swedish scientist, arranged for me to attend a Soviet conference in Alma Ata. On the map, the topography around that part of Kazakhstan looked promising for trout, if they existed in Central Asia, or at least some variety of cold water fish. Rows of mountain ranges successively climbed behind the city towards elevations of over 20,000 feet at the border of Sinkiang province some 150 miles distant, as the crow flies. Numerous rivers were seen to flow down into the huge lakes below Alma Ata in the Kazakh steppe.

So I packed a brand new fly-fishing outfit in anticipation of finding free time to explore the area and, perhaps, to discover salmonids, in an area remote to western anglers. Little did I suspect the obstacles that were to appear.

The five-hour night flight from Moscow was packed. As the plane circled Alma Ata in the May dawn I was immensely pleased to see the snow-capped mountains, the deep green forests, sparkling rivers, and attractively laid out small city.

The conference went well. The numerous banquets with endless toasting in Armenian brandy became somewhat wearing, also on the liver. I looked forward to the weekend and asked my hosts for information on fishing and hiking in the mountains. I was met with a mountainous inertia; the term "stone-walling" comes to mind. The blank looks, the massive procrastination now are understandable. Some of the most important Soviet rocket and missile facilities were in those mountains. I was probably suspected to be a spy, and angling was a feeble excuse.

I wheedled and cajoled, but the answers were, "The authorities do not give fishing permits to foreigners," "The fishing areas are too remote," "There are no fish." The cumbersome bureaucracy of the Soviet system was performing its most effective task, blocking any action that might involve individual responsibility. As a minor example, when I wished to swim in the Alma Ata municipal pool, I was refused because I did not have a Soviet swimming certificate. You needed a license even to swim in that country!

Finally, I was able to talk my hosts into arranging a hike into the mountains, accompanied, of course, by an official of the conference. This had been cleared with the KGB agent assigned to the meeting, a shifty–eyed Latvian. The country was beautiful. A series of ridges rose toward the snowy mountain peaks. Alpine meadows were dotted with wildflowers and interspersed with stands of evergreens and birch. Rivulets ran down and joined ever larger streams. I spotted small fish that could be baby browns but never had the chance to find out for sure. So ended my piscatory ambitions.

The conference ended. A week-long caravan to Tashkent, Samarkand, and Bokhara was superbly organized, the food and wine thoroughly enjoyable, even the ceremonial *Koumiss*, the fermented mare's milk of the descendents of Genghis Khan.

Before returning to Moscow I presented the brand-new fly fishing outfit in gratitude to my Kazakh host, himself a quiet rebel aginst Moscow's rule. His Mongolian features broke into a smile. We both laughed heartily.

Spanish Fly

"Q UIERO UN PERMISSO DE PESCARE." I tried out my bad Spanish on the fish warden I had tracked down in the local *Taberna*. He looked at me, amazed. This was the sacred time to enjoy a meal and siesta. One does not do business between two and five in the afternoon. But, reluctantly, he made out the fishing permit. I got no information on where to fish, though. His digestion was more important.

My new wife and I were in the town of Reinosa, high in the *Cordillera Cantabrica*, near the headwaters of the *Rio Besaya*, which flowed north for thirty miles to empty into the Bay of Biscay. We were in northern Spain on a vacation trip from Switzerland. The VW camper had carried us through Bordeaux, Marseilles, Barcelona, and Burgos. The main destination was Santillana del Mar at the mouth of the Besaya, from where we planned to visit the caves with prehistoric paintings, such as *Altamira*.

But trout fishing was on the agenda, and here was an opportunity. Willy-nilly, I drove along the stream looking for promising water. The small river had riffles and pools with abundant overhanging vegetation. The water was cool. We stopped and picnicked by a deep pool. I unlimbered the rod and tied on a streamer since I saw no surface activity. I let the fly swim near the tail end of the pool and a swirl and flash near the fly brought my heart to a standstill.

"That was a tremendous rise," I exclaimed to Manisha. I cast again and the same thing happened. This was no ordinary trout. This was a monster. Just then, a man appeared on the other side of the river. He took one look at me and started shouting something. I caught the words *"salmón"* and *"prohibido."* It gradually sank in, to my deep disappointment, that I had strayed onto a salmon spawning stream, very likely onto the redds. I reluctantly retrieved the fly, cast a wistful look at the river, and we continued our journey. What would have happened, I mused, if that man had not appeared. I might have hooked, in my ignorance, the biggest trout of my life.

CHAPTER 6

Swiss Watchers

Switzerland! The oasis of security and peace in a troubled world. A sabbatical leave there in 1975 led to a long-term stay beginning in 1978: I had a challenging job at a physics research institute, akin to the work I had done in Los Alamos. I needed frequent escapes from the ivory tower atmosphere of physics and technology. What better than fish? But Swiss officialdom kept a close eye on me.

IN OVER FIFTY YEARS OF FISHING I CAN COUNT ON ONE HAND the occasions that a warden checked my license. That is, if I exclude my six years in Switzerland from the tally. And one of those checks nearly landed me in the pokey.

It started when we first moved to Switzerland in 1975 and decided to live in Bern, the capital and in the center of the country. The encounters with Swiss authorities began with a visit to the *Fremdenpolizei*, the officials that regulate the activities of foreigners. They could not believe that we wanted to live in Bern, when I worked at the Swiss Cancer Research Center in Lausanne and Manisha studied for her diploma at the Jung Institute in Zürich, each over an hour away in opposite directions by train. Scarcely any Swiss, it seems, travels more than a few miles to and from work.

These crazy foreigners from America, the *Polizei* must have said, to travel over two hours each day is *verrückt!*

But otherwise we were left alone. Eventually the itch came to drop a line in the water. It was stimulated by seeing large trout rising to mayflies on the Aare. This river encircles the high, narrow peninsula that is the ancient site of the walled town of Bern. I studied up on the rivers and fish of Switzerland.

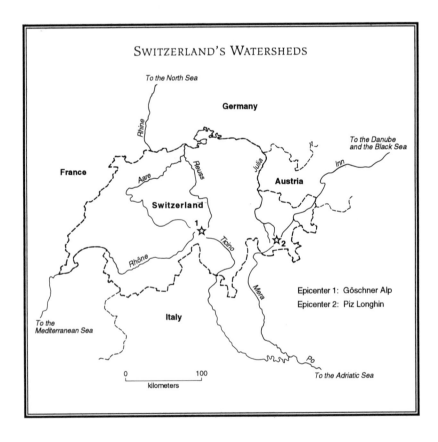

The Swiss Alps form the center of water drainage for most of the western European continent. There are two epicenters of drainage: one at Piz Longhin, 2645 meters high, near the Maloja Pass; the other some thirty miles west in the Göschner Alp, near the head of the Rhône glacier.

The first epicenter divides the rainfall into three watersheds: one into the River Inn, thence to the Danube and the Black Sea; the second into the River Mera, to the Po and on to the Adriatic; the third into the River Julia, to the Rhine and to the North Sea.

The epicenter in the Göschner Alp splits into three watersheds: one into the Rhône and the Mediterranean; the second into the River Aare; the third into the Reuss and on to the Rhine; the fourth down the River Ticino and into the Po.

I found it interesting that in this way rain falling over a small part of the Alps can eventually end up in the North, Mediterranean, Adriatic, or Black Seas.

And there is plenty of water from that precipitation. I added up the figures for all the drainages; the mean annual drainage rate out of Switzerland comes to 1526 cubic meters per second. That is equivalent to nearly seven million gallons of water per second, day and night, all year long.

Watching the early summer run-off from the Alps, I fantasized on how to divert even one day's worth of that water to some rain-poor region of the world. My mind boggled at the magnitude of the task. Some minds are pondering problems like that, because increasing population pressures are going to demand solutions.

Eventually I was able to fish five rivers in three of the four watersheds; the Aare, Reuss, Emme, Inn, and Mera.

I started after painfully relearning some German in order to communicate with a friendly tackle-shop owner in Bern. His tips led me to get a license and to begin the exploration of the highly recommended Emme which, yes, flows down the Emmental into the Aare.

Emmental is one of the most beautiful valleys of Canton Bern. It is rolling pasture land in the lower elevations but assumes a wilder character closer to its origin in the Alps. The large solid Bernese farmhouses fit naturally into the landscape. Green pastures blend into forests that climb up the surrounding ridges. The cows complete the picture postcard with their large, initially quaint, later annoyingly noisy bells. The cheese bearing the name of Emmental tastes best when consumed by the banks of the Emme with a glass of local wine and a crusty loaf of local bread. To top it off, the upper Emme is all that a fly fisherman can wish for, clean water, rapids, riffles and pools. The stream is manageable by wading and the occasional covered bridge pleases the eye.

I began fishing the lower stretches just below the town of Hasle. In the spring there were heavy hatches of Mayflies that attracted many fishermen to the Emme. I often needed to share a stretch with three or four other fly fishermen. The rest of the year was uncrowded and I rarely saw another angler.

During the hatches, which I recall were mainly olives and March browns, the dark Cahill was effective. But Swiss browns were quite demanding, requiring an excellent presentation and a fine leader before they deigned to accept the imitation. For the number of rises at the height of a hatch, which was almost like a cloud, very few trout were fooled by my imitations. That made it very challenging indeed.

Few of the trout were heavier than a pound but they were beautifully colored and fat—like the nearby cows.

As everyone knows, Switzerland is a well-run small democracy. The Swiss are meticulously honest. I was thus astonished by the number of times my license and catch were checked, or, as they say, *kontrolliert*.

One day, after a good morning's fishing, with three keepers for our evening meal, I walked upstream, reconnoitering for future outings. A local rustic, complete with pipe, greeted me and began, pleasantly, to discuss the weather. Noting my broken German, he switched from Bernese dialect to *Hoch Deutsch*. The conversation got around to fishing. He asked, mildly, *"Haben Sie etwas gefangen?"* To which I proudly replied, *"Ja, drei schöne Forelle."* He smiled and asked, *"Bitte, könnten Sie mir diese zeigen?"*

I was flattered and proudly took out the trout from the back flap of my jacket. In a twinkling, my erstwhile farmer friend whipped out of *his* jacket a measuring device and his identification card. Urs Meyer was the local *Fischgewächter*.

Nonplussed and slightly shocked, I handed over the fish. He measured their lengths and I breathed a sigh of relief; they fulfilled the twenty-four centimeter (about ten inch) size limit. But that wasn't all. He inspected my fishing permit and examined my tackle to make sure I had no double or treble hooks and then politely said *"Bitte leuge"* and went his way. That was the subtle approach.

Another time I was fishing the Reuss just below Mülligen in Aargau. It was on a broad stretch of riffles and pools with an undercut bank that promised to have trout. The water was fairly high, the tail end of the runoff from the Alps, and I had luck with a streamer, killing two good browns in an hour and stowing them in my jacket. I noted a figure approaching who looked and acted, this time, like a game warden. The perusal of the fishing permit completed, he asked me something in dialect. This time the communication was essentially nil. I could not understand him. The query, I thought, was if I had seen other fishermen, to which I replied, *"Nein, keine."*

He went off and I resumed my fishing. About an hour later I hooked my third brown, killed it, and took out the fish bag from the jacket. With a shout the man jumped out of the nearby shrubbery where he had been lying in wait, and grabbed the fish from me. A long tirade in dialect ensued as he measured them. They were legal. A further tirade was countered by my spluttered protests about, *"Einen Missverständniss."* I breathed a long sigh of relief when it seemed that I would escape arrest for giving false testimony.

The man had chatted with a spectator who saw me catch the previous fish. He assumed I covered up because they were under-sized and therefore lay in ambush to catch me in my crime. There were further muttered threats which I imagined ranged from deportation to jailing before the man, frustrated from not finding any incriminating evidence, went away to pester other fishermen.

My many other encounters with Swiss authorities were unremarkable.

Getting permission to fish in Switzerland, and for that matter most of Europe, can be complicated, and expensive.

Canton Bern and some smaller mountain cantons have simple requirements—one permit applies to all the waters of the canton. Others not. For example, in Canton Aargau where we lived during the last years, I had to buy the cantonal permit which was required for all but only provided very limited public water. I then had to buy permits for specific stretches of water from holders of the local fishing rights. These originated in the Middle Ages and still belong in many places to the hereditary riparian owners even though they no longer own the land by the water.

The *Privatfischenz-Pächtkarte* for a particular stretch of the Aare near where we lived had to be obtained from a grumpy old woman in a run-down cottage. She reminded me of the old woman in the shoe. The regulations read like a legal document; wading was *verboten*, fishing from a boat or island was *verboten*, this and that was *verboten*. Angling in Switzerland isn't simple.

A favorite stretch of the Emme was near the village of Goldbach, famous for its cider. It is subalpine terrain and the river is smaller, wilder, and boulder-strewn as if transplanted from some high mountain stream in the Rockies.

On a Friday evening I would drive up the Emmental from the N1 *Autobahn* which traverses Switzerland, cross a covered bridge and turn off into a narrow, nearly imperceptible track through the dark forest. The campsite was on the edge of the woods, a few yards from the river, with high cliffs looming on the opposite bank. At dusk a fire warded off the chill and cooked the meal. The darkness closed in, the murmuring and chattering of the river became more apparent. All else was still.

At first light I donned the waders and explored the water. No rises, no insects, only a thin mist on the water. A hare's ear nymph, cast upstream, would do.

In the deep water close under the cliffs were large boulders creating all sorts of hydrodynamics. Pools, eddies, and thick tongued torrents divided the granite monoliths. The nymph landed on the steep slope of a rock, slithered down and disappeared into a pool.

The leader telegraphed the twitch from the attack of a hungry fish. I abducted the rod by controlled reflex, not too little, not too much, and the connection was established.

The fish breached and revealed a broad flank with bright red spots. Its steady boring dive into the fast water forced me to slip and slide downstream to get below the heavy brown.

My heart thumped as I cautiously brought it to the shore, netted and released it—a bright, fat, three-pound native of Canton Bern. For once I had done everything correctly, just like the Swiss.

CHAPTER 7

The Revenge
of the Fishgod

I do not consider myself a religious person. The worship of Nature is as far as I go. But some experiences have been numinous, have led to thoughtful introspection , and have made me more humble. Near-death experiences often do that. The Hindus believe that God reigns over a well-structured army of lesser dieties. Since the experience I relate here the Fishgod has been in my thoughts whenever I fish. I believe I have become a gentler and kinder fisherman.

ONE DAY THE FISHGOD DELIVERED A FORCEFUL REMINDER of my misdeeds against his kingdom. It happened like this. I spent several days one September with my good friends Bertil and Ingela on the west coast of Sweden, some twenty miles south of Gothenburg. Bertil's ancestral home is a lovely eighteenth century manor, a short walk from the rocky coast of the Kattegat.

Bertil was also an enthusiastic fisherman, and one cold, rainy morning we went cod fishing. He had a favorite spot far out from the shore where an underwater reef lay across the tidal current. We anchored just downstream from the reef and jigged heavy metal lures off the rocky ledge. The cod were actively feeding and Bertil and I hauled up a good mess of fish.

The cod family (*Gadidae*) is ubiquitous throughout the North Atlantic and includes a freshwater relative, the turbot. The common cod is variegated brown on its dorsal surface and has a white belly. It may grow to huge proportions but because of the heavy commercial fishing pressure usually weighs up to ten pounds. The fish that we caught ranged from three to five pounds.

The cold weather bothered Bertil's hip so much that he was laid up for several days. I was so enchanted, however, by the surroundings of the low rocky coast and numerous islands that I resolved to go out alone.

The next day was also cold and rainy but I was determined to fish, not realizing what fate had in store. I borrowed the boat. Because I enjoy rowing, the outboard motor was not mounted. The row to the reef was about one kilometer.

I began to fish using the same technique as the previous day. I boated a few cod. Presently I brought up a new kind of fish from the depths; a beautiful golden, green, and violet fish with a long spiny dorsal fin. It resembled a tropical fish, out of place in this cold, grey part of the North Sea. Perhaps a messenger from the depths, which, in the Indian fairy tale, swallowed the golden ring of the princess, thus creating fateful consequences.

The fish was dangling on the hook, its spines menacing, but I had no forceps to remove it from the hook. Gingerly I unhooked this newcomer, but in the process had one spine prick the middle finger of my right hand. Within seconds a burning pain began at the puncture site and began to spread up the right hand. I sucked the wound, which bled freely, but with no relief, and began to realize this was more than a prick.

The pain worsened. Within minutes the finger and hand began to swell, and the comprehension grew that this was indeed a serious problem.

I hoisted anchor as best I could, and tried to row back to shore. Soon the pain and swelling became so severe that the right arm and hand became useless. I was about a half kilometer from shore—dizzy, faint, and helpless.

About 200 yards away, however, a pair of men were fishing from a skiff. I called out and waved my good hand. They waved back. This went on for a while until they gradually realized that something was wrong. They motored over and I tried to explain my predicament, pointing to the fish lying on the floorboards. One of them exclaimed in horror, "*Herre Gud, en fjärsing!*" The name meant nothing to me, then. Their faces registered extreme concern. A towline was immediately bent on and I was towed into Röda Holmen (Red Harbor) at maximum speed.

By the time we arrived I was in total agony—helpless, shivering and perspiring. They drove me to Bertil's house where Bertil immediately recognized the situation, took charge, transferred me to his Land Rover, and drove to the small hospital in Onsala. As we came in the door I collapsed, was placed on a gurney and wheeled into the treatment room.

An intravenous drip of saline, calcium gluconate, and decadron was started. I was given intramuscular demerol and my right hand and arm were placed in a bowl of very hot water (the poison is a protein that can be denatured by promptly applied heat). However, the time lapse of over an hour was too long, and the pain and swelling persisted. The wedding ring on my right ring-finger was cut off because of the edema. Finally, after two hours the pain and swelling began to recede and after three hours I was able to leave with Bertil's help.

I was thoroughly exhausted from the experience and it took several days to recoup strength, weeks for the pain and swelling to diminish, and months, with the help of physiotherapy, for the middle finger to become functional again. To this day, many years later, that finger has not regained its full strength or range of motion.

Never have I experienced such pain. Even with medical experience the severity was beyond my imagination.

Thus the Fishgod struck me down, as with a bolt from Zeus, and nearly succeeded in terminating my onslaughts on his Kingdom.

His messenger, the weever fish (*fjärsing* in Swedish), or *Trachinus draco* in the family *Trachinidae*, lives along the coastal waters from West Africa, throughout the Mediterranean, to the Atlantic coast waters off Spain, France Britain, and Scandinavia. The name "weever" apparently originates from the north-eastern Old French word, *wivre*, meaning viper or dragon. The anterior spines on the head contain a heat-labile poison capable of producing severe pain, shock, and respiratory depression. Some cases of death have been reported among fishermen, probably related to exposure in isolated locations, such as could have happened to me.

The poison is hemolytic and local tissue necrosis can develop in untreated cases. The pain produced is excruciating, more then that inflicted from stingrays. There is a case report of a commercial fisherman amputating his own finger because of the intense pain (I can believe it!). Despite its venomous aspects the weever fish is not poisonous; it is edible and said to be highly delicious. Back in the seventeenth century, the English poet Drayton wrote, "The Weaver, Which although his prickles venom bee, By Fishers cut away, Which Buyers seldom see." However, at that time I was in no mood to sample it.

Since that momentous day I still fish but have become far more caring, gently returning the prey to its watery world, and retain only the occasional specimen for the dining table.

I have taken that event as a portent. My transition to a fly fisherman has become nearly complete and, as primitive hunters are said to do, I now utter a short prayer for the quarry.

CHAPTER 8

A Patch of
Wild Strawberries

Ingmar Bergman's early film "Wild Strawberries" was titled
in the original Swedish 'Smultronstället.' This translates to mean
the place or patch of wild strawberries. In the film, the old doctor,
Isak Borg (played by Victor Sjöström), has many disturbing dreams
of his past. In the final dream of the film, however, he looks down
from a sunny hillside upon the idyllic scene of his childhood home,
complete with a family picnic and the little boy fishing by the lake.
As Ingmar Bergman describes it in his autobiography, The Magic
Lantern, Isak Borg's troubled features suddenly soften, he becomes
quiet and gentle, there is a moment of grace. The word 'smultronstället' connotes the secret place associated with one's fondest memories, the real or symbolic place where one can return each year to
gather the wild strawberries unknown to anyone else. That is what
Isak Borg rediscovered in his dream.

I HAVE SUCH A PLACE. This tells about how I found it. My new job was in Los Alamos, high up in the Jemez mountains of northern New Mexico. Coming into a community of physicists, engineers, and biologists was a heady experience intellectually, but also, at 7200 feet of elevation, barophysiologically.

Once adapted and the dizziness gone I began to explore the surroundings. To escape into the surrounding nature was a reaction to the highly technological project in which I participated. Bill Black, new-found friend, colleague, raconteur, pathologist, and fly fisherman, provided enough descriptions of the canyons and streams, abetted by free-hand drawn maps, to make exploration of this geologically fascinating area easier.

The Jemez mountains actually originate from one gigantic volcano that blew its top millions of years ago, leaving a large central crater or caldera. It is odd that the site of this ancient explosion is only a few miles from where Man, with his fatal ingenuity, developed the first atomic bomb with all its consequences.

Tens of thousands of years after volcanic activity had diminished, a lake began to fill the crater. Eventually the lake water broke through the walls of the caldera and carved several river canyons, thus draining the lake to the present fertile plain of over twenty miles in diameter. This is now called the 'Valle Grande' and is nearly 10,000 feet above the sea.

I started to explore the canyons and streams originating in the Valle Grande. One of the canyons was carved by the present Rio San Antonio, which flows south to join the Rio Jemez which in turn joins the Rio Grande just north of Albuquerque.

The lower stretch of the river flows through arid land dotted with mesquite, chaparral, and aspen. It is flanked by buttes and cliffs of volcanic origin with brilliant hues of ochre and cinnabar. The ascent from the base of 5,000 to the headwaters over 10,000 feet high gradually unfolds an alpine landscape bedecked with deep green meadows dotted with wildflowers, and forested with conifers and other evergreens. It is splendid western high mountain country.

The San Antonio is not a large stream, perhaps fifteen to twenty feet wide at midsummer and wadeable up to the knees with occasional and unexpectedly deep holes. It has two outstanding qualities that make it attractive to the fly fisherman: a rich mineral content due to influx of water from hot volcanic springs near its origin (the dissolved minerals support an abundant aquatic ecosystem); and it is *not* stocked in the upper stretches by the New Mexico Fish and Game Commission. Thus occasional fishermen and vacationers tend to leave untouched a "wild" population of brown trout. These were introduced many decades ago and have superceded the native Rio Grande cutthroat (*Oncorhynchus virginalis*), possibly because of the higher water temperatures generated by the hot springs. But browns are also far more wily than cuts and thus tend to prevail under competitive conditions.

During that year I camped and fished along the San Antonio, the Jemez, the Baca, and other streams, and came to love the peaceful, unpopulated country. The San Antonio became my favorite.

After the year in Los Alamos I moved to Switzerland. Piscatological explorations continued in rivers such as the Aare, Reuss, and Emme, but my thoughts often returned to New Mexico and the San Antonio.

Switzerland, to many, is an idyllic country, an island of peaceful prosperity in this troubled world. It contains some of our most beautiful mountain scenery. Yet, after the initial period of enchantment with its beauty, order, and efficiency I sensed a vague unease, a feeling of constraint. Eventually I realized the origin of this feeling—it was the limited space in relation to population, very much like in Japan. It was psychological as well as physical. The mind could also be hemmed in. There were few places one could go without seeing Man or the signs of Man: well-manicured trails, huts, cows with bells, direction signs, all very neat and pleasant, but constraining.

New Mexico (and the American West) was different, with vast vistas and few signs.

Thanks to the continued linkage of the programs in New Mexico and Switzerland it was possible to return yearly to New Mexico. Following the work week I would spend weekends camping along the San Antonio. The drive from Albuquerque would lead north ninety miles through Bernalillo, the Zia and Santa Anna Indian Reservations, Jemez Pueblo and Jemez Springs, to La Cueva and thence to the end of an old dirt road alongside the stream.

After setting up camp, generally just a lean-to, I would explore the waters slowly and thoroughly, gradually working up from the flat, open, shallow riffles in the alpine meadows. Small, naïve browns lay along the banks, rising to terrestrial insects such as jassids, ants, and grasshoppers. In the evenings, hatches of various mayflies enhanced the variety of piscine activity. With a light rod, a long leader, and a low profile, the upstream fly casting was often rewarded by rises from interested, sometimes imprudent trout. Numerous feisty and colorful denizens were hooked and released. A single poor cast, however, would quench activity for a considerable time.

I scarcely ever saw another human being, much less that special breed, an angler. The occasional elk or beaver at dusk were my shy and distant companions.

The San Antonio tumbles down from the Valle Grande through a narrow, steep canyon, several miles in length. Here lies the greatest challenge of the river. Big and wily trout lurk in their deep holes, coming out to feed when it suits them, selectively, on the abundant surface and subaquatic life. I was never fortunate to be there at the time of a big stonefly hatch but Bill Black vividly described it. Big browns would throw caution to the wind at the height of the hatch and a well-placed imitation often resulted in a dramatic battle, but often lost to the fish because of the small stream, underwater rocks and snags, and the quick-wittedness of the big trout.

Without a hatch in progress the task was harder. Generally the first cast over their lair was the only chance to arouse their interest. Subsequent casts usually flogged the water and put all neighboring fish down. Casts often had to be made around and even over midstream boulders. There were plenty of hangups on the backcasts due to, the narrowness of the stream, its tortuous course, and the abundant streamside vegetation of alder bushes, firs and pines. The well-placed cast was often rewarded, however, with a take from a good ten-incher, and a precarious battle of wits up and down stream.

By wading, often just wearing shorts and wading shoes, I could learn and memorize the topography of the stream-bed: the deep holes, the best trout lies, the unproductive stretches. Wading slowly upstream, I would often dislodge a startled trout from an unsuspected lie which was not apparent from above the stream surface. I would be as startled as the trout. Thus "reading" the trout water with the eyes was enhanced by "treading" with the feet.

There has been controversy over the possible ecologic damage to the stream-bed produced by wading. I was aware of this and observed what my boots would dislodge as I waded. With fairly good sized rocks and boulders there appeared to be little effect. In this stream, the underside of nearly every rock was crawling with a menagery of insects and crustaceans in various stages of development. They seemed happy and undisturbed by the overhead size eleven wading shoes. In the gravel beds at the tails of riffles some dislodgement occurred. I developed an "ecologically sensitive" approach to the problem—to wade only where the essential cast was needed, and to cast as often as possible from dry land. Wading, of course, may signal the angler's presence to the fish by sound transmitted through the water and the creation of wakes in quieter stretches.

It is obvious that an army of anglers can produce ecological damage, not just to the stream beds but also to the banks. The damage produced by the occasional angler is quickly repaired.

(The peasant common sense of the Swiss has considered this decades ago. The licenses sold are often in several classes, the cheapest, with a larger quota, often prohibit wading, while the very limited and more expensive licenses permit wading).

As one ascends the San Antonio, the canyon becomes steeper and mountaineering techniques are needed to scale the gigantic boulders that choke the narrow gorge. Although the holes are deep in this section, they contain few trout, or at least few that revealed themselves to me.

The canyon then becomes gradually wider and less steep. The topography of the stream changes; it becomes again a classic western trout creek with gravel bed, boulders, broken down beaver dams, log jams, amd crystal clear water.

It is a trout's paradise and a fly fisher's challenge. This is a favorite abode of large browns, hiding in the shadow of a tree or rock. Despite dextrous side-arm casting under, over, and around fallen trees and piles of driftwood, my fly caught on a branch or trunk half of the time.

One day I cast a large weighted Montana nymph into the swirl just above a fallen trunk that led into a deep pool formed by an undercut bank. The lure sank into the pool and a vigorous take startled me enough to nearly drop the rod. The trout was, for that stream, a monster. It led me a merry chase around the pool and all its snags. The light rod was scarcely suited for this task, but the hair-fine leader held and eventually he was netted—a fine fifteen-incher.

My slow exploration of the San Antonio led one day up past the gorge to a bend in the river around which I saw a spectacular sight: the towering brick red cliffs of the outer edge of the ancient crater loomed above; beyond, the canyon suddenly widened, bisected by the now peacefully meandering stream bordered by alpine meadows. At the bend, one meadow was encircled by willows, aspens and firs to form a small natural amphitheater. From this meadow I could look upstream to see the red cliffs now glowing like fire from the light of the setting sun. Above was translucent dark blue through which pierced the distant cold light of Venus. It was a vision of unbelievable beauty. A natural harmony of the setting transmitted equanimity straight into the soul.

There was instant recognition. This was my *smultronställe.* Fishing suddenly seemed of less importance, perhaps more an excuse to achieve the few moments of transcendence one may be fortunate enough to experience in a lifetime. Like Isak Borg, I smiled.

I returned to camp and the next day, using the topographic map, found a dirt road that brought me within reasonable distance of this place of my dreams. I packed in the gear and set up camp in the small meadow.

The predatory activity was chastened. I spent hours simply being there, doing nothing.

The six rules of Tilopa, the Tibetan Zen master, state:

Do not think, do not imagine, do not analyze.

Do not meditate, do not reflect.

Abide in the Natural State.

I obeyed them.

That night, near the embers of the campfire, snug in my sleeping bag, I listened to the gentle gurgling of the nearby stream, and watched the magic of the shooting stars.

It was a moment of grace in that small spot in the New Mexico mountains.

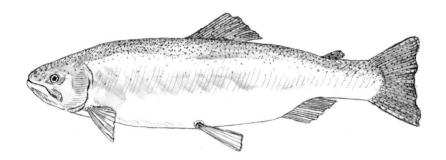

CHAPTER 9

Farr Inn on Horton Plains

Trout Near the Equator

In 1984 I relinquished the heady directorship of a medical research project in Switzerland for a job at nearly the opposite end of the world—and of the medical spectrum. My WHO assigment was to work in a run-down cancer hospital on the outskirts of Colombo, the capital of Sri Lanka, the new political, religiously provocative, and uneuphonious name for Ceylon. In addition to setting up a clinical program I was charged to develop an academic and practical training program in clinical oncology for Sri Lankan doctors. Nearly all of the cancer specialists had left the island for political or economic reasons. The brutal war between the Tamil separatists and the Sinhalese was escalating. Tourism was moribund. But the countryside remained dramatically beautiful and there were trout in the mountains. As always, I carefully packed my fly rod and fishing gear.

THE TRAIN CHUGGED SLOWLY UPHILL FOR THOUSANDS OF FEET, leaving behind the steamy heat of Colombo. Manisha and I luxuriated in the perceptibly increasing dryness and coolness. Dark green jungle changed to miles of rubber plantations, diagonally scarred trees in strict geometric order, then rolling hills of tea bushes with scattered shade trees. Tamil women, with baskets strapped to their backs, patiently, carefully, plucked the terminal leaves of the tea shrubs.

Tea, the epitome of Englishness, demands labor intensive industry. In Sri Lanka, the industrious Tamils continue to do much of the hard labor, inevitably conflicting with the more leisurely and seigniorial Sinhalese in the power struggle that has brought this beautiful island, the so-called Pearl of the Orient, to its political and economic knees.

But we were now figuratively and literally above the problems besetting the country. This was to be a much needed vacation in the highest habited area of Sri Lanka, the Horton Plains, named after a former colonial governor. Far in on Horton Plains was Farr Inn, also named after an old colonial.

We disembarked with baggage and fishing gear at an elevation of nearly 6000 feet, in the tiny hamlet of Pattipola, which consisted of the railroad station, a few houses and huts, a small store and a toddy shop. No vehicles were in sight. We had been told that there would be no problem finding a car to take us up the final 1000 feet to Farr Inn. What to do? The station master was sympathetic but of no help. There were no phone lines to Farr Inn. My copy of the venerable *Murray's Handbook for India, Pakistan, Burma and Ceylon, 1962 edition*, the former bible for travellers in this area (now superceded by the *Travel Survival Guides* and similar books) stated that Horton Plains were reached from Pattipola "by foot or on horseback: distance 6½ m." There were no horses here either. We were not prepared for the walk with cumbersome luggage and a steep climb.

I wandered over to the toddy shop where a group of very happy men were enjoying the aromatic beverage. Toddy is the indigenous drink of the island. It is made from the natural fermentation of the sweet nectar that forms in the crevasses of sprouting palm leaves at the top of tall toddy palms. Most paraplegics in Ceylon and South India owe their fates to falling out of the trees while collecting the toddy. From my experiences at one hospital in Neyyoor, Kanyakumari District, I learned that over half the hospital beds were occupied by these tragic cases. The accident rate is probably high because many of the men are drunk on the toddy that they sip during the tree climbs.

I was warmly welcomed and offered a glass of toddy, a pleasant tasting effervescent brew about as potent as strong beer. The ambience and beverage reminded me of pleasant lunches in Switzerland during the grape harvest when freshly fermenting grape must, locally called "salser," was traditionally imbibed. I would have liked to tarry but had a desolate wife waiting at the station.

We exchanged the usual pleasantries and fact finding that every Westerner gets.

"Where is your native place?"

"How many children are you having?"

"Do you like our country?"

To which I gave the answers. And I found out similarly about my hosts.

After a suitably polite interval I got around to stating our problem.

"Ah, that is no problem. We have a jeep to take us back to the factory (tea estate). You can ride with us!"

I gratefully accepted their kindness and hurried back to tell Manisha the welcome news. Eventually, the jeep appeared. We clambered into the back with our baggage. A jeepload of happy souls, several of whom, including the driver, had two sheets to the wind, took off on a hair-raising climb along a narrow, rutted, and potholed road. We drove through a thick forest of gum and acacia—great leopard country—and emerged onto a wide grassy plateau dotted with copses of trees, the Horton Plains, at an elevation of nearly 7000 feet. It was getting dark and chilly, and big drops of rain began to fall. We felt eternally grateful to our saviors who refused all offers of compensation.

Farr Inn has the dimensions of the typical large British colonial dak bungalow or rest house. There was a central dining room, opening out upon a porch with adjoining bedrooms, a small library-sitting room, and the kitchen and servants' quarters to the rear. Each bedroom was blessed with a fireplace, which was used every night as the low clouds swept over the plain releasing cold, driving rain. There was a gasoline-powered electric generator that ran a few hours each evening to supply dim, flickering light to the dining room and bedrooms. Mostly we were to rely on kerosene lamps.

The evening meal was the usual colonial relic, ubiquitous even to this day throughout the ex-British colonial world in old-fashioned hostelries catering to the Westerner: a tasteless creamed soup, an overcooked breaded slab of fish, a piece of mutton with potatoes and a limp vegetable, concluded by a trifle or a pudding. Ceylonese beer was a salvation. We gave pointed instructions to the chef to provide Ceylonese meals for the remainder of the stay.

Gusts of wind and rain rattled the windows as we retired to the bedroom with the cozy roaring fire in the fireplace. We enjoyed a good night's sleep under blankets, the first such opportunity since arriving in the country.

The early morning sun revealed a fresh green dewy landscape of rolling moors with gently waving patana grass, dotted with buttercups, gentians, and rhododendrons. After breakfast I took the short walk to the forest ranger's office. The chief ranger was helpful and told me much of the local terrain and wildlife. A topographic map showed the meandering course of the Belihul Oya stream which I would fish. It originates on the slopes of several nearby peaks in the Totapola, flows across Horton Plains to plunge downhill at World's End, a precipitous outlook over the southern coastal plain. We later hiked there and looked down thousands of feet to the humid, misty jungle below. It would have made a splendid launching site for a hang-glider.

Elephants no longer inhabit the high hill country, but sambar, the large Asian deer with a characteristic bark, leopards, and monkeys occupied the forests adjoining the plain.

I paid for the fishing permit and was joined by a game guard, a requirement of the local regulations. The permitted fishing stretch covered five miles of water. My guard was a pleasant young Sinhalese who also was helpful to me in advising on flies. With Rohan's smattering of English and an appreciation of fly patterns we were able to communicate satisfactorily.

I began to fish at the first big pool near the inn, the Leg of Mutton Pool. Wherever I have fished in the Anglophilic world I have noted a predilection to name pools of well-known fishing streams. The pool very vaguely resembled the shape of a leg of mutton, I would rather have called it the Lamb Chop Pool.

My very first cast was rewarded with a vigorous take of my nymph, right in the surface foamline streaming down from the small waterfall. I was so surprised that I nearly dropped the rod. The fish took off down the pool, jumped twice, and was off—with my Hare's Ear nymph in his mouth! I inspected the end of the leader and cursed quietly.

When, oh when, would I learn to tie knots carefully? The leader had not broken; it had unravelled from the eyelet of the fly!

The brief commotion had put down the fish in that pool. I watched for surface insects but there were none. I decided to continue downstream, trying nymphs and streamers along the way. In a small pool, fed by yet another waterfall, I connected, this time with a green sedge nymph, and landed a fourteen-inch rainbow. The stomach contents revealed that the current diet was small crustaceans, snails, black beetles, and, yes, green caterpillars.

I spent the remainder of the pleasant sunny day exploring the rest of the stream, enjoying the packed lunch with beer, and spotting and hooking a half dozen more rainbows, keeping two in all for dinner. My guard-cum-guide approved the partial catch-and-release policy.

The Belihul Oya was a small stream—what we would call a creek. It could almost be called a spring creek, because much of the water released to the stream is filtered through the spongy patana grass roots that form a layer of many feet over the underlying reddish laterite clay. Thus the heavy downfalls are buffered by this huge sponge extending for miles in all directions. This spongy action also prevents erosion, of which I saw very little. Farther upstream, in the protected part of the stream, I saw gravel beds that could well serve as redds for spawning.

The Belihul Oya was a pleasant stream to fish but lacked variety. It was essentially a series of small waterfalls and pools. There were few rapids and no boulders or other obstructions creating interesting currents and pockets. Wading was scarcely necessary because of its small size. I am sure that farther downstream, in the coastal plateau, it would take on the dimensions and variety of a challenging fly-fishing stream. But no trout would survive those warm waters. Perhaps mahseer would be there, though, provided they had not been poached to near-extinction as has happened in most of India.

I remember well the beautiful streams shown in David Lean's film, "The Bridge over the River Kwai." Those scenes were shot in Sri Lanka, in the jungle below Horton Plains, and certainly included the Belihul Oya drainage.

I later learned more about the history and propagation of trout in Ceylon. As in most British hill stations the nostalgic colonists tried to reproduce the conditions of their homeland. This included trout fishing. The streams around the nearby station of Nuwara Eliya were first stocked with brown trout fingerlings in 1882. They had been hatched from fertilized ova packed in ice and brought from England in the month long sea voyage to Colombo by determined anglers.

The hatchlings thrived in the new environment. A brown trout of fourteen pounds was captured several years later. However, they failed to reproduce.

Further attempts were made, but it was only when rainbow ova were imported from California's McCloud River in 1899 that successful, although limited, natural reproduction occurred. The strict requirements of the right gravel and water conditions for natural propagation have made exotic transplantation to the equatorial regions generally dependent upon fish hatcheries.

The hatchery at nearby Bamberakelle continues to raise rainbow trout for the benefit of the few trout anglers in Sri Lanka and for the future hoped-for return of foreign tourists.

That evening we enjoyed a trout dinner that was prepared under my hawk-eyed supervision. It was not overcooked, as is the sad fate of most fish dishes around the Western world. Perhaps even the Fishgod would have approved.

CHAPTER 10

Naked in Nyanga

In 1988, the World Health Organization asked me to travel to Zimbabwe. The new government health service, with no specialists in my field, had requested help to develop a a training program. This was a fascinationg challenge and I began by studying the country's history, geography, and the background to this problem. I learned that the former Rhodesia was wrested from the Shona and Matabele tribes barely 100 years ago by Cecil Rhodes and his motley army of mercenaries. But Rhodesia is no longer ruled by the white tribe. For over fifteen years Zimbabwe has been a part of the new black Africa. In contrast, however, to next door Mozambique, which was in political, economic and social shambles, Zimbabwe's Robert Mugabe allowed the whites to retain their commercial and agricultural holdings, and many of their civil appointments, thus helping to preserve the preexisting governmental and commercial infrastructure of the country. This happened despite the preceding bloody and brutal civil war between the whites and blacks.

Thus, only one-half, rather than all (as in Mozambique) of the white population of 200,000 left Zimbabwe. And many are returning—because there has been no blood bath since independence, and it remains a beautiful land with a healthy climate, rich in resources. They even retain their privileged enclaves. The Eastern Highlands is one, whose damp cold evokes ancient memories of woad-painted ancestors. So when I arrived in Harare, the capitol, the Nyanga region of the Eastern Highlands tugged me like a magnet, for here are forests, lakes, streams, and trout.

IT SEEMED LIKE SCOTLAND. The barren mist-shrouded moors were interspersed with forests of scotch pine. In the hotel there was a roaring fire in the sitting room hearth, and others in the bar and dining rooms. The game room had a sink, scales and blackboard with columns for date, species, weight, and fly that lured the trout to its brief moment of fame.

It was the cocktail hour and the barroom was crowded with tweedy men and flowery women, some drinking whiskey, others pink gins. Only the topographic maps on the wall and the fez-festooned Shona retainers dispelled the illusion. The scene was in the Rhodes Nyanga National Park, located in the Eastern Highlands of Zimbabwe. This was Africa.

"It's a frightful mess. The scotch pines are spreading like weeds. The native vegetation hasn't a chance!" His mustachioed red face framed a glass full of amber liquid. It was an old story, heard again and again around the world, a disastrous forestation scheme using an exotic species. There followed a long list of other things gone wrong since independence. But my bar companion eventually concluded in his clipped regimental voice, "At least I'm alive and here. Wouldn't be anywhere else. Can't afford to complain too much. And there's plenty of good trout hereabouts. Let me show you some spots." We went over to the topographic map on the wall.

The first time I traveled to the Eastern Highlands was with hired car and driver. A corpulent, silent Shona man, Cyril Ngomo gave me the security of knowing the way, negotiating the military road blocks, and driving skillfully on the wrong side of the road (from an American's viewpoint).

It turned out that I could have easily managed on my own—which I subsequently did. The roads are excellent and the traffic sparse.

I enjoyed the 130 mile drive from Harare (formerly Salisbury) to the Eastern Highlands. It begins on the high central plateau, passes through scattered towns and extensive farmlands, and, in the last twenty miles, rapidly climbs through hills with dramatic rocky bluffs, lakes and woods. The bracing mountain air can be felt as the destination is reached at an elevation of 1840 meters (6000 feet).

The Rhodes Nyanga Hotel is cosily secluded in forests of jacaranda and eucalyptus on a hillside overlooking Mare Lake. A rambling one-story bungalow with extensive lawns and beautiful gardens, it is the former residence of Rhodes. His presence lingers—on the long verandah where I sat, he must have enjoyed breakfasts in the soft, dewy mornings reminiscent of England.

The pleasant Anglo-Rhodesian couple who owned and managed the hotel welcomed and got me settled. My chauffeur was given a comfortable room. Then a walk to the nearby park headquarters for the fishing license and maps. The African chief ranger and the blonde, female assistant ranger supplied me with necessary information and gave the taste of how Zimbabwe was now being run.

After tea, I drove up the Mare River to the fish hatchery. It straddles the cold, clear stream, so necessary for the propagation of salmonids. And there, staring me in the eye, was my old friend, the American Brook Trout—correctly speaking the char, *Salvelinus fontinalis*. In other rearing tanks were rainbows and browns.

I have read that in most exotic locations around the world where the conditions permit and where the British settled in, enterprising

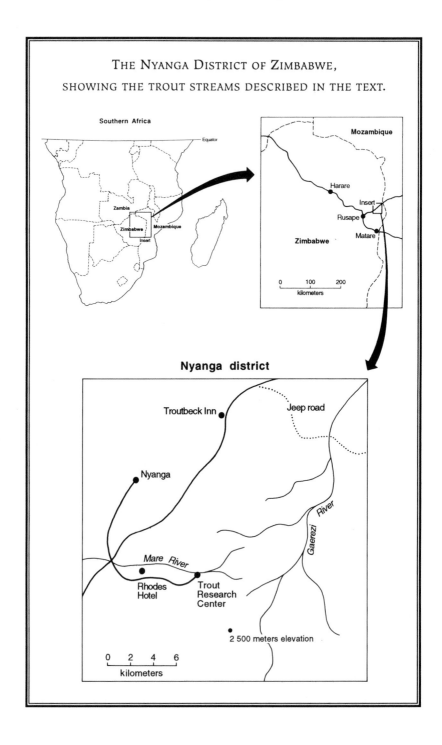

THE NYANGA DISTRICT OF ZIMBABWE,
SHOWING THE TROUT STREAMS DESCRIBED IN THE TEXT.

pioneers painstakingly introduced their beloved native brown trout followed by the very adaptable Pacific Coast rainbows. Their efforts, beginning with the clipper ships in the 1860's to Tasmania and New Zealand, later in Asia, Africa, and South America, should someday be lovingly recorded in a book.

But I was surprised to find brookies here. Even in the States they are not often hatched for put-and-take angling. Brookies are very finicky in their reproductive requirements and embryonic development. The water must be consistently less than sixty degrees as well as extremely clean. Both rainbows, and even more, browns, are more tolerant of warmer temperatures.

The trout-rearing and -stocking programs seemed to be well run. The angling regulations in the National Park were surprisingly strict and thorough. Non-weighted and non-spinning flies only, if you please! The open season is 31st October to 31st May, Zimbabwe being in the Southern Hemisphere. License holders are required to send their catch reports to the park ecologist annually.

In the detailed brochure describing the trout rearing I found two fascinating vignettes.

The first one stated that a coloring pigment, "Carophyll Red," was added to the fish pellets. This improved egg production and fertility. The same pigment was used in the production of the soft drink "Fanta." I mused on the implications of this bit of trivial pursuit. What if human beings responded like trout? Doctors would be prescribing large quantities of Fanta for barren mothers. Countries concerned about overpopulation might ban it.

The second item was the statement that male trout were kept upstream from the females in the rearing tanks during the spawning season. The reason was that hormones released by the females stimulated the males and caused excessive fighting and injuries. How vulnerable we males are to feminine wiles in so many different forms!

I learned that all three exotic species cannot reproduce naturally in Zimbabwe despite the elevation, water purity and temperature. The problem lies with the spawning beds. The texture and abundance of gravel is key to salmonid and char spawning. I had heard about this problem in India and Sri Lanka. Trout fishing in and near the tropic latitudes seems fated to remain largely artificially supported, an exotic sport for exotic (from the Greek *exotikos*, from outside) branches of humanity.

The following morning, in the predawn darkness, I took my fly rod and walked down to the Mare River, really a creek. On the way I startled, and was startled by, a Dik-dik, a small deer, which bounded off into the cold, foggy gloom. Crouching low by the stream I saw the trout moving upstream from their daytime lair in the lake. Fishing a small streamer supplied by my host, I readily hooked several rainbows and killed one to bring back to the game room for the traditional weighing in and for breakfast.

But I was keener to explore the back-country of Nyanga where remote seldom fished streams were numerous. That evening my host introduced a local resident, John Weeks, who offered to take me the next day to the Gairezi River.

John is a true pioneer. Originally from London, he served in the Metropolitan Police. When Ian Smith's Rhodesian government capitulated to pressure to allow unrestricted elections, a large contingent of British bobbies was sent down to supervise the election process. Both sides of the struggle had accepted them as a neutral and peace-keeping force. After the election, many decided to take a risk and stay on in this beautiful land. John was one, and he bought a house in Mutare and some undeveloped property high up in the Nyanga hills. Over the years he cleared the land, planted orchards, and built a house. He, his wife, and two strapping sons and a daughter learned Shona, became Zimbabweans, and thrived in the new environment. A tall, muscular man, John is a no-nonsense, enterprising builder of the new country.

The following morning I drove up to their ranch. The two sons took me in the Land-Rover through dense pine forests over a deeply rutted dirt road, past Shona villages with the typical conical huts, gradually descending into a valley. The purplish-blue hills of Mozambique appeared on the horizon.

Finally, at an elevation of 1900 meters, we reached the Gairezi. It was a river of my dreams. Of course, I have seen many rivers of my dreams, but each one is special and belongs in a separate dream. I just felt joy in seeing and feeling the wonderfully clear cold current sweeping down a valley flanked by rocky buttresses, copses of gnarled trees, and huge boulders. No one was in sight, nor was there any sign of habitation.

The boys dropped me there and proceeded on with an assignment to collect certain types of rock for building material. I slipped into the stream in my shorts and hiking shoes and commenced to wade upstream. The river was beautifully wadeable except for the scattered deep holes of translucent turquoise which appeared to be over twenty feet deep. The river bed was sublimely clean gravel and rock, a condition that I have seldom seen in fishing forays in Europe and America but did again experience in New Zealand and Chile.

The insect life, however, in this rather barren but beautiful dry landscape was sparse. The river valley was on the lee of the crest of the Nyanga range and had a scanty rainfall. Therefore the trout were few, scattered, and large. They fed on terrestrials and minnows.

John had given me some beautifully tied Matuka streamers for these conditions. I continued to explore upstream without seeing a trout until I came to the first large pool.

There, in the shade of an overhanging boulder, I glimpsed the familiar shadow of a large trout, gently finning in the slight current. Gingerly crouching and creeping up on the opposite bank, I placed myself to be able to cast across the pool and allow the Matuka to sweep by the trout. The first cast was too short. The trout had not stirred. The next cast was good and the fish moved out of his position and leisurely engulfed the artificial. I carefully set the hook with a sideways motion of the rod and felt the weight and power of the rainbow, for rainbow he was when he leaped, clearing the surface and landing with a tremendous splash. The battle proceeded with acrobatic tail-walking and finally burrowing down into the depths, where a convenient sunken tree stump became my undoing, or more aptly, the fish's undoing of the strand that had connected him to me.

I reeled in and sadly examined the broken end of the three-pound test leader that I had optimistically but injudiciously tied on, perhaps directed by the Fishgod's admonitions.

After that it was as if the tension had been broken. I fished on, but more with an eye to my surroundings, absorbing the feel of the place. I saw no more trout as the sun rose to the apogee and the heat raised a slight sweat. Finally, with my stomach signalling for sustenance, I stopped by a spacious deep pool surrounded by gigantic boulders, stripped, and plunged into the cold aquamarine depths, emerging chilled and refreshed.

I warmed myself in the sun, carefully shielding the sun damaged skin of my face with a Zimbabwean wide-brimmed floppy hat, but allowing the rest of my body to soak in the infrared, ultraviolet and whatever other rays that were available. Lazily, like a sun-warmed lizard, I slowly dressed to resume the quest, but my heart was no longer for the chase.

The Gairezi had become one more *smultronställe*. It, too, often appears in my daydreams and fantasies about whisking away when necessary on a flying carpet to utopian enclaves where beautiful streams bring peace and tranquility.

CHAPTER 11

Baptism in the Tongariro

In 1990 I was offered a job as temporary consultant at the Auckland Hospital in New Zealand. I accepted the post partly in order to fish. I did my work conscientiously, faced some challenging medical problems, and came to know and like the sometimes reticent but always friendly Kiwis. Limited to a day's drive from Auckland, I concentrated on the streams draining into the immense Lake Taupo in the middle of North Island. My experiences may be useful for anglers and other visitors. But beware the mighty force of the crystal-clear Tongariro river. I learned—the hard way.

"WE ARE SHORT A CONSULTANT. Can you help us out?" John Probert let this bombshell drop in a very New Zealand offhand way. Could I? The prospect of a new clinical experience coupled with the pleasure of fly fishing for North Island lunkers was a heaven-sent opportunity that I could not refuse.

I had called John, an old friend and colleague in Auckland, from my Massachusetts home, for suggestions about a remotely possible holiday fishing trip to New Zealand. Little did I expect the possibility of a busman's holiday. My patient and understanding wife, who had her own practice to deal with, granted me clearance.

The necessary red tape was processed in the next several months: temporary medical license, staff appointment at the Auckland Hospital, work permit and visa. It was really quite easy in New Zealand, in comparison to many countries that look with deep suspicion on foreign doctors wishing to practise, even temporarily, on their hallowed if sometimes flea-bitten soil.

I decided to bring an eight-weight rod in order to deal with big waters like the Tongariro and the potential double-digit weights of the Kiwi browns and rainbows. I assembled a mini-fly tying kit to absorb my time and interest during the long lonely evenings to be spent when not fishing or doctoring.

The flight from Boston to Auckland was one of the most delightful, comfortable, and forgettable of the many tedious long-distance flights that are the price to pay for the travel itch. It demonstrated the one outstanding virtue of economy coach travel: retractible armrests. Neither business nor first-class permits the passenger to stretch out across three unoccupied seats as is possible in the lowly tourist class. I was lucky to be in a half-filled plane. Except for the two or three meals of the fifteen hour 12,000 mile one-stop flight, almost all in darkness, I was able to stretch out completely and doze or sleep the time away.

The approach to Auckland in the rosy dawn of the overtaking sun showed a city that reminded me of two others—Stockholm, festooned by a lovely archipelago, and San Francisco, bright and wind-washed, with many hills.

John collected me at the airport and settled me in at the medical officers' quarters of the Auckland Hospital, the large teaching hospital for northern New Zealand. The room was cozy, neat and clean, with a balcony that overlooked the harbor.

For the rest of the day I explored the city, a compact and manageable place. The Aucklanders walked briskly, were polite and friendly to a stranger, and had an initially incomprehensible accent, akin to the Australian. I discovered many book shops and music stores, and noted an active concert program. An economical long-term rental of a small Datsun completed the preliminaries.

John had invited me to dinner that evening. The directions were complicated, and I soon got lost driving in the dark. My previous experience with left-hand driving was nearly thirty years before in India, where very little vehicular traffic had made it easier, and safer, to learn. After negotiating one of the numerous traffic circles I noted headlights coming straight at me and realized with horror that I had emerged by habit onto the right hand lane. Quick reflex evasive action avoided a crash and I drove on, shaking with visions of the near disaster on my first night in New Zealand.

At a stop signal someone rapped hard on my side window.

The face of an obviously angry man was staring at me. I lowered the window.

"What's the matter with you, mate?" he shouted. "Are you drunk? Get out of there!"

The driver of the car I had confronted head-on had turned and followed me. So I would also have a baptism of Kiwi fisticuffs to celebrate my first day! I got out while using my best American accent to explain my one-hour-old experience with left-hand driving. Luckily for my facial features, he quickly calmed down and presently was explaining the directions to John's house. We parted the best of friends. In New York or Los Angeles I would have probably been shot.

The consultancy started the next day and I gave the job my fullest energy. Teaching young residents and medical students has always been fulfilling. The patients were pleasant and obliging, similar to my Swiss patients who tend to project an omnipotence upon physicians. If they really knew! But then they, like many Americans, would be anxious and insecure about their medical management. No easy answer.

But before dawn the following and nearly every Saturday, my full attention turned to that sacred quest for the Piscine Grail—the ultimate experience of fly fishing for the wisest and biggest trout and catching it. The car packed, I headed south in the darkness to Taupo Moana, the Maori name for the Sea of Taupo, 240 square miles of lake in an ancient caldera.

The drive was relaxing (after I had adapted to the left-hand lane) and scenic. The countryside of rolling green hills, orchards, fields with sheep or cattle, reminded me of northern California and Switzerland. Only the unusual trees with dramatic silhouettes and strange flowers and shrubs indicated the true location.

The traffic was light and the roads good but narrow. Danger, however, lurked even in this rural Eden.

One rainy morning, without any warning, an approaching car blithely turned across my path within braking distance. I slammed on the brakes, skidded into the opposite lane (luckily there was no following car), and came to shaky halt by the side of the road. I jumped out and, now in my turn, rapped on the window of the culprit's car, now stopped in front of a convenience store. In it were five big and burly Maori men. My suddenly feeble protestations evoked a good-natured and ethanolic response, "No harm done, mate. Have a drink!" A can of Steinlager, New Zealand's Budweiser, was thrust out the window. I gracefully declined.

The other Taupo trips were thankfully troublefree. The dawn crept up to melt the morning mists and give a glimmering sheen to the dew-fresh countryside. Occasional rainfalls and even a touch of snow (June is New Zealand's winter) freshened the landscape and deepened the greenness.

The final lap of the 150 miles southwards brought me over the rim of the ancient caldera 2000 feet in elevation, to a breathtaking view of Lake Taupo and the surrounding snow-clad volcanic range. Here was the feeding ground for the exotic browns and rainbows. Energetic New Zealanders had introduced them in the last century from fertilized ova carefully preserved on ice for the long sea voyages of that era.

I have read that the browns came to New Zealand via Tasmania from England in 1867. The rainbows came from the Russian River, north of San Francisco, in 1883. They were, in fact, steelheads (anadromous rainbows) and steelheads they have remained.

The lake, full of small indigenous eels and later introduced smelts, became the ocean for these fish. It provided a nearly unlimited dinner. The primal instinct to reproduce led them to seek the gravel beds of the numerous streams flowing from the surrounding volcanic countryside down into the lake. The conditions were right for spawning; no significant predators, water of utmost purity and ideal temperature, and gravel of the right consistency.

Trout rarely have had it so good!

So, naturally, they grew and grew and grew. Once the secret was out, anglers came from all parts of the world. Zane Grey was an early enthusiast, calling New Zealand the anglers' El Dorado, thanks also to the abundant sea fishing.

All this I had learned by assiduous reading, benefitting especially from the beautifully written books by O.S. Hintz, who lovingly described the Taupo region. Much more in New Zealand, of course, is a fisherman's mecca, but I concentrated on Taupo because of its reputation and convenient access from Auckland.

At the risk of spoiling the place for regulars, I must mention a small oasis for fisherman in Turangi, a small village at the southern end of Lake Taupo. Turangi calls itself, modestly, the Trout Fishing Capital of the World. The Creel Lodge is run by a laid back New Zealander and is a delightful retreat of housekeeping cabins on the banks of the mighty Tongariro River, of which I have much to say. Because the Tongariro came close to achieving my premature demise.

After checking in that first cold rainy morning, I hastily rigged up to give the river a try. A pair of baggy featherweight stocking foot waders was part of my kit. I neglected, however, the basic precautions of bringing along a wading staff and of cinching the opening of the waders, both necessities for exploring unknown big waters.

I slipped into the river just below the Judge's Pool, a long smooth run, with the intention of downstream streamer-fishing into the next lower pool. The clarity of the water and cleanness of the boulder-and-gravel river bed were striking. The current strengthened as I gingerly waded out. I thought that this was a remarkably strong current for the so-far modest depth. In fact, my eyes were deceived by the clarity of the water.

Before knowing it, I was in trouble. It was at a point where the slightest increase of water pressure would dislodge my precarious foothold on the underlying boulders. In the act of turning to retreat to the safety of the shore, my dorsoventral surface perforce faced the force of the current. It was enough to levitate me off the stream bed. I was swept downstream into deeper water. Without footing, I toppled and the waders promptly filled with icy Tongariro water. I became a sort of water-filled balloon. This was it! A fly fisherman's fate!

Luckily, with water up to the shoulders, I touched river bottom and a series of hops brought me to the shore just above what I later learned to be the Groyn (gorge) Pool.

Ignominiously, I crept out of the river, completely soaked, feeling like a half-drowned rat. And noting a group of Maori anglers on the opposite bank having a good laugh did not help my self-esteem.

Thus ended the first ten minutes of the first day of fishing. A baptism indeed! The Fishgod's minions of Taupo Moana nearly succeeded again.

Even in those serious straits, however, I had kept a firm grip on the fly rod as I did all those years ago. In fact, I lost nothing but my pride, the fly boxes being safely zippered away.

After a full twenty-four hours to recover and dry out, I was game to give the Tongariro another try, but far more cautiously this time. And far wiser. I later read this passage about the Tongariro from Hintz's *Fisherman's Paradise* (Reinhardt, London, 1975). "Generally the river calls for deep and sure-footed wading. It surges and spills over a boulder bed. It is a river to be fished with a good deal of respect; over the years it has claimed more than a few lives."

I sought the help and advice of the owner of the tackle shop next to the Creel Lodge. Frank Harwood is a dour, taciturn New Zealander. I sensed in him a wide-ranging knowledge of things piscine and riverine and promptly engaged him to guide me for a day, not to fish but to show and teach me all about the lower Taupo region.

It was an unforgettable day. In his beat-up station wagon we drove to a multitude of larger and smaller streams, trudged along the banks, observing the holding places, the stream conditions, and the distribution of the migrating fish. The lush vegetation and varied bird life added to the enjoyment of the day.

But Frank never smiled. He had a gloomy view of life. It had rained the previous day and night. The water, to me, was slightly tea-stained but still clear. Not so to Frank. " The water is dirty!" No use in fishing under these conditions! To me the water was far clearer than most that I have waded in on many continents.

Frank showed me the New Zealand flies and gave me tying tips and materials. My tongue rolled over the classic New Zealand names: Parson's Glory, Mrs. Simpson, Craig's Nighttime, Jack's Sprat, Taupo Tiger, Kakahi Queen. Most were streamer flies with the matuka pattern.

But a revolution in fishing technique had recently occurred. The new approach was upstream nymphing. The flies ranged from the traditional Gold-ribbed Hare's Ear nymph to the artificial salmon egg.

The usual rig was a heavily weighted nymph at the point and a lightly weighted or unweighted dropper fly. Local fishing regulations permitted fly fishing only on most streams, with no added weights on the line. But weighted flies were permitted; thus the openly accepted subterfuge.

The rivers and streams that Frank introduced me to that day emptied into Lake Taupo along its eastern and southern shore (see map). In clockwise order we visited the Waitahanui River, Hinemaiai Stream, Tauranga-Taupo River, Waimarino Stream, and finally the Tongariro, the largest river of all, supplying forty percent of the lake's water.

Most of the surrounding land was Maori property and I received instructions as to when and where to obtain permits to traverse their lands.

It would be too ambitious to describe the waterways that I saw that day and explored over the following weeks. However, let me give the flavor.

The water quality, as I said, is remarkable—crystal clear, drinkable, with no evidence of algal formation due to contaminating phosphates. The stream beds and banks are formed from the detritus of volcanic rock, and range in texture from fine pumice sand to large boulders. The surrounding vegetation is lush and green, flax, broom and lupins, blackberries and brambleberries, ferns and reeds, poplars, pines, eucalyptus, and the ubiquitous manuka, a smallish prolific evergreen, an excellent and aromatic source of firewood for cookouts.

The birdlife was prolific. The small chubby fantail is one of the friendliest birds I have encountered. It flutters around in a fussbudgety way. It seems to like human company. The native kingfisher, grey warbler, and silvereye were less common. Several introduced species including finches and thrushes added to the beauty of sound and sight. Not so the starling.

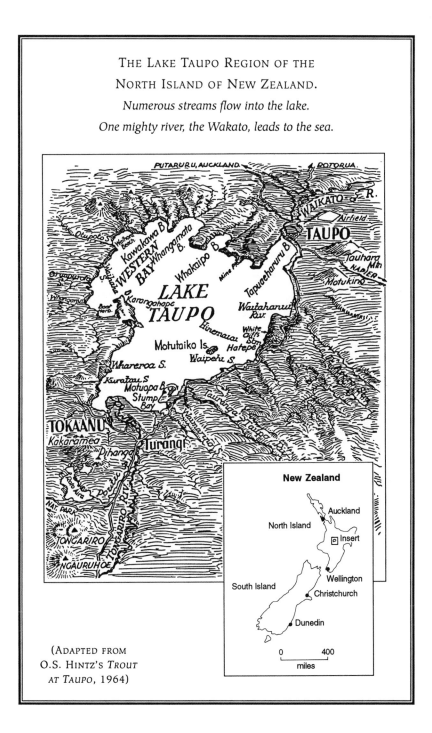

THE LAKE TAUPO REGION OF THE
NORTH ISLAND OF NEW ZEALAND.
Numerous streams flow into the lake.
One mighty river, the Wakato, leads to the sea.

(ADAPTED FROM
O.S. HINTZ'S *TROUT*
AT TAUPO, 1964)

The streams, depending upon the rate of descent towards the lake surface, present all forms of hydrodynamics. Near the lake they may be quite tortuous with slowly meandering currents. Further upstream the pace quickens and rapids, pools, and waterfalls delight the eye and the fishing arm. The Tongariro was special—a mighty river with powerful currents which had forcibly baptised me into the fellowship of the Maori god of Taupo Moana.

During my stay I saw few insects, this being the New Zealand fall and winter. I was told that dry fly-fishing was good in the summer. Rises to some New Zealand insects were rather special, such as to the green beetle. Ephemeras (mayflies), midges, and caddis are seen in spring and summer. There are some fresh-water crustaceans such as small craw-fish (koura) but I did not see any myself. It seemed that the principal food source was smelt in Lake Taupo and that there was not a large holdover population in the feeders. Thus the fishing during the spawning run was similar to that for salmon, steelhead, and sea-run browns, a matter of enticing them to strike, not necessarily imitating any recognizable creature.

Well, what about the fishing? I was afaid someone would ask.

It is difficult and demanding. These are not dumb, small, stocked trout. They are big, four pounds and up, wise and wary in their upstream journey through crystal clear and often shallow water. I found that the slightest mistake—a poorly cast fly, an inadvertent movement within their line of vision, or a heavy tread on the stream bed—would send them off in a flash.

I estimated that I expended twelve fishing hours for each fish, or more positively, three fishing hours per pound of landed trout.

I learned a lot about fishing and about New Zealand, and developed a very tired right arm in the process.

The first fish came easily, none thereafter. When Frank dropped me off at the Creel Lodge after the long day of riverine reconnaissance, there was enough time for a try on the Tongariro. I pulled on the waders, assembled the rod, and drove south several miles upstream to the Whitikau Pool which he had shown me early in the day. At least two anglers had had hook-ups as we looked on earlier that day.

When I reached the spot there were still anglers in the water and I decided to move up to the next pool, called the Fence Pool, which was empty of fishermen. This was a fifty–yard–long stretch with a rapid at the head and shallows at the tail. It was dusk, with little time left to see where to cast. I tied one of Frank's matuka streamers on a seven-foot leader attached to a sink-tip floating line and cast to the far bank in order to allow the fly to swing down and across the riffle at the tail of the pool.

The first cast was decisive. A sudden stop of the swing induced the reflex sideways abduction of the rod and a heavy fish was on, dour, not breaking surface but boring deep and sideways. It must be a brown! The battle persisted until my arm ached and the quarry reluctantly showed itself. A steelhead! A scarred and somewhat lean five pounder, it was a female that had just spawned, a few eggs remaining in the roe sac. I proudly displayed the fish to a New Zealander who had observed the action. " Not bad, mate!" He did not appear very impressed. Little did I know of the difficulties ahead.

I made the Tuesday predawn drive back to Auckland in time for morning rounds at the cancer center. The remaining working days revolved around consultations, clinics, and conferences. Patient procedures such as biopsies, implants, and radiographic studies gave satisfaction. A few problematic cases tested my mettle and competence.

To this day, after over forty years of clinical practice I am still surprised that so few problems are similar. I must constantly mull, ponder, cogitate in the attempt to pull the proverbial chestnut from the fire. Wisdom in medicine must come eventually; so far it has largely evaded me.

One weekend, one of my new colleagues, Barry Evans, a Welshman turned Kiwi, joined me in Turangi. Barry gave a knowing Welsh wink, "We'll catch a limit!"

We concentrated on the Tauranga-Taupo. This is close to the ideal trout stream. Not too small or too large, wadeable except for deep holes, good gravel and sand bottom, plenty of casting room and plenty of holding spots (including snags).

The water was low and clear. No rain had fallen for nearly a week. I saw a pod of three big trout in tandem, finning along an undercut bank in two feet of gin-clear water.

Slowly and painstakingly I moved to a strategic casting position some twenty-five feet downstream. With excruciating caution, I false-cast the floating line until the nymph dropped two feet to the side of the hindmost fish. It plopped and the fish scooted like greased lightening. Disappointed, I fished on. Veteran Kiwi anglers later informed me that I should have waited for the pod to regroup and then have tried again. One should patiently stalk a known quarry rather than blindly search. More efficient that way. I continued upstream casting, with not another fish sighted all day.

We were skunked! So also were two of Barry's New Zealander friends. I did not feel so badly after that. Such can be New Zealand angling. The fish may be big but they are wary and often far between. They migrate in groups. The fortunate angler encounters them in the right conditions, such as after a fresh spate, or in a holding pool.

For example, one morning during another visit I explored the lower stretch of the Waimarino after an overnight rainfall. The pool was about a quarter mile from the stream outlet on Lake Taupo. The stream level had risen but the water was clear. There were some dark torpedo shapes in the depths of the long pool. I cast a weighted pheasant-tail nymph on the dropper to the far bank and allowed it to drift. The floating end of the leader suddenly halted, I twitched the rod, and the fish was on! The to and fro battle ranged the length of the pool (from where did the term *playing* a fish come?) Eventually I landed the deep-bellied, gorgeously colored steelhead, obviously just arrived from the lake. It was a memorable day and I prepared a memorable meal at the Creel Lodge for Barry and myself according to the following Kiwi recipe:

TRUITE TAUPO

INGREDIENTS

1 large, whole trout

2 shallots, finely chopped

4 Tbsp. butter

¼ cup cream

⅓ cup white wine

Salt, pepper, thyme, lemon juice

Lightly sauté the shallots in the butter, pour ¼ of mixture on bottom of baking dish. Season trout with salt, pepper, and thyme and lay on top of shallots. Add rest of mixture over trout. Bake in 375° oven for 20-25 minutes or until the flesh over backbone is opaque and flakes off.

Remove trout to hot platter.

Deglaze pan with wine and cream. Strain resulting sauce into small saucepan, reduce slightly over medium flame, add some lemon juice.

Pour sauce over trout and serve.

A New Zealand white wine or Australian chardonnay is essential to complete the gustatory experience.

By late June the weather was cold and wet. A few hiking trips in the volcanic country around Taupo were reprieves from my obsessive single-mindedness. I bathed in the sulphurous Ketatahi hot springs, high up on the slope of Mt.Tongariro (6500 feet in elevation). It was refreshing, but I smelled like a rotten egg.

The day I flew home from Auckland John asked me how I liked the stay. "John," I said, "if you want me again just pucker your lips and blow."

CHAPTER 12

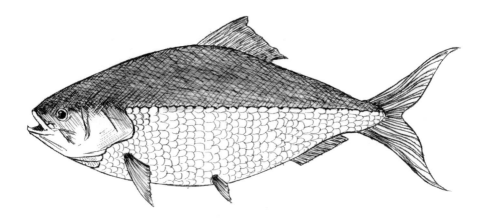

In Praise of Shad

After our return to the United States in 1985 we settled in
Massachusetts. I soon heard about the splendid revival of a great
game fish, the shad, on the Connecticut River. I have made pil-
grimages each spring to the hot spot at South Hadley.

"THE POOR MAN'S SALMON," it is called. I agree. Having paid
ninety or more dollars a day for a guide on salmon rivers in
Nova Scotia, I find it a pleasant and economical contrast, here in New
England, to share the egalitarian shad fishing scene on the river bank,
cheek by jowl in a line of rough-looking, pickup-truck driving, red
necked, baseball-cap-wearing fishermen. Each of us cast shad darts
far out into the roily spring runoff. Knowledgeable anglers know the
sweet spot. For them, nearly every cast ends with a strike and a prolonged battle with the broad-sided, tough fighting shad.

This field of battle is the Connecticut River just below the Holyoke
dam in South Hadley, Massachusetts. The resident license fee is sev-

enteen dollars and fifty cents, good for a year, and the average spinning outfit costs forty dollars. No thousand dollar cane rods here, thank you very much!

I discovered that in colonial times the number of shad running up the Connecticut were estimated to be six million each spring. Then along came industrialization and thus dams, which stopped the hormonal imperative to breed. The shad run declined to a pitifully small fraction of the original figures. And not just shad—the salmon run has never recovered.

The Holyoke, Turner's Falls, Vernon, Bellows Falls, and Wilder Power Station dams are the remaining barriers on the Connecticut to the upstream migration of anadromous species such as salmon, shad, herring, striped bass, and sea lampreys and to the downstream migration of the catadromous eels. These stations have, however, erected fish by-passes that now permit considerable numbers of fish to complete their annual spawning migration. The shad run in 1992 was over 700,000.

In the spring when the river water temperatures reach fifty-five degrees, schools of shad begin their spawning run up rivers all along the east coast of the United States and Canada. Since their transplantation in the last century, the same occurs along the Pacific coast.

My interest in shad is two-fold: the first is the pleasurable duty to fill our freezer to brimming so that Manisha and I can supply us and our friends with nearly a year's worth of delicious Bengali fish meals. The shad is a close relative of the *hilsa* which migrates up the Ganges and its tributaries each spring. The *hilsa* is prized among Bengalis and ranks with the *rohu* as a delicacy.

My second interest in the shad is for its challenge in fly-fishing. Like the salmon, the shad apparently do not feed during their spawning migration. Why they strike at lures is not clear. Most experts consider it to be instinctive aggressive behavior. The mating instinct can bring out crazy actions in all of us.

The traditional lure is a weighted, garishly painted lump of lead on a hook. The "fly" must also be a lure or attractor, as are all so-called salmon flies. They are not entomological imitations.

The shad is single-minded in its spawning quest. It hugs the main channels but probably rests in pools and eddies. The lure must be fished deep. The fly fisherman therefore uses streamer techniques with sinking lines and short leaders. The lure must seek river bottom to be effective, and therefore lost terminal tackle is to be expected. The take is usually at the end of the drift and at the beginning of the retrieve. Expect a real battle on a rod for seven- to nine-weight line. My estimate is that, pound for pound, a shad has about one and a half times the battling capability of a salmon, thanks in part to its flattened ovoid shape.

I find it exciting to fish by canoe in the turbulent rapids below the Holyoke dam. Careful boat handling is necessary to avoid swamping. The best location is just above the drop-off into deep holding pools. As with salmon fishing the water can be covered by quartering casts using suitable weights of sinking line with added lead-core leaders if necessary. The anchor line is periodically lengthened until the hot-spot of milling shad is located. Only occasionally do shad reveal themselves by breaking the surface.

The strike is often subtle but immediately a strong battle begins, enhanced by the current and the oblate shape of the fish. They rarely breach, resorting rather to power tactics, "bulldogging" against the angler until exhausted, often a battle of ten to fifteen minutes. Most fish weigh four to five pounds. The record shad caught by rod was about eleven pounds.

When I first visited the scene at South Hadley, the singular behavior of a majority of the fishermen struck me with astonishment—they threw back all the fish into the river. I asked some of them why, half expecting to hear them proudly voice the new American ethic, catch-and-release. This, despite the count of 721,336 shad at the

Holyoke fishway in 1992.

No. The answer was, in general, "You can't eat shad, they're full of bones."

It would break the heart of a Bengali to hear those words. The delicacy of the Ganges rejected for having too many bones! Yes, the shad has a lot of bones, but they can be dealt with in a number of ways.

The first is to fillet out the bones. Boyd Pfeiffer in his classic *Shad Fishing* (Crown, New York, 1975) provides an illustrated guide to boning the fish. It is by no means easy. But once that chore is accomplished, the delectable fish can be prepared in many ways. One good recipe, adapted from Pfeiffer's book, is as follows:

CHARCOAL BROILED SHAD

INGREDIENTS

boned shad fillets (for 4 persons)
½ stick butter
juice from ½ lemon
1 tsp. crushed capers
1 Tbsp. grated onion
2 cloves garlic, ½ tsp. powdered crushed
cayenne pepper
salt and fresh-ground black pepper to taste

Melt the butter and mix in all the ingredients. Baste both sides of the fillets with the mixture, and broil over medium hot coals. A special fish holder to turn the fillets without breaking is very useful. Garnish with lemon wedges and parsley, and serve with saffron basmati rice.

An Australian or West Coast chardonnay will enhance the marvellously delicate taste and texture of fresh shad.

A second method of avoiding or minimizing the bones is to cook the shad slowly. Boyd Pfeiffer has several recipes that he claims will make all the small splinter bones disappear. This involves steaming or low heat for at least five hours. I have not tried this but have my doubts about the resulting taste and texture of the fish.

The third method is simply to ignore the problem of bones. Any properly cooked fresh fish will flake away from the bones. So too with the shad. Any fish lover knows how to deal with bones. The taste and texture are at their best in a freshly caught whole fish.

A word about shad roe: to many, this is the only worthwhile edible part. Yes, shad roe is excellent and there are numerous recipes. To my taste, the roe is too rich for a main course and, like caviar, is best served as hors d'oeuvres. Freezer-cold vodka or akvavit are excellent lubricants.

The hilsa, cousin if not twin to the shad, is prevalent in ocean waters around India, but is best known in Bengal where it is fished in the delta of the Ganges and Brahmaputra Rivers. Like the shad, it belongs to the herring family (*Clupeidae*) which also includes sardines, alewives, and menhadens. David Starr Jordan in his classic *American Food and Game Fishes* (Doubleday, New York, 1904) notes that most species of this large family inhabit all the seas and usually swim in immense schools.

As an exotic parody of Izaac Walton's masterpiece, John Masters, an Indian Army officer and father of the late modern novelist of the same name, wrote and illustrated *The Compleat Indian Angler* (Country Life, London, 1938). He describes the hilsa in the following dialogue between Piscator (Izaac Walton) and the author.

"What are those men doing in the river, and how can they be floating in the river so long ?" (asks Piscator).

"They are fishing for hilsa, and are supported in the water by an inverted chattie" (a raft supported by inverted jars). "The hilsa is a seafish and he runs up the big rivers to spawn about this time, when

the snow water is coming down. Now you can see the net. It is a triangle at the end of a long pole. The fisherman pushes the pole right down underneath him, and holds it there till a fish strikes the net, when it closes by itself, and he hauls it up to the surface, and transfers the fish to the bag he carries around his waist."

"I would prefer to fish for him with an angle. What does he take?"

"So far as I know he has never been caught on rod and line. But his habits have never been properly studied. Fishing is a wholetime job, as you know, and we, in India, can only do it in our spare time, so we only touch the fringe of the subject. When I left India the scientists were still trying to discover whether the eggs of the hilsa sunk to the bottom or floated down to the sea to be hatched. I ask you, what the hell does a hilsa come hundreds of miles up the river for, if the eggs aren't going to be hatched out there? There are millions of them running up the river now, as they have done every year for centuries, and we know nowt about them. What a country! You wait till you get your teeth into that hilsa, Izaak; he's extraordinary good eating, very richly flavoured and tasting something like a mackerel. He runs to about fifteen pounds and has the build of a fighter, so should be good sport if we only knew how to set about it."

Apparently Lieutenant Colonel Masters did not know about the similarity of the hilsa to the American shad, or of the sport fishing known even then.

Regarding shad breeding, Jordan states, "Single fish have been known to yield from 60,000 to 156,000 eggs, though the usual number does not exceed 30,000. The eggs are very small, semi-buoyant, and require six to ten days for hatching, the time varying with the temperature of the water." In the warmer temperatures of the Indian rivers the hatching time is probably shorter.

It is interesting that Jordan, in 1904, states, "The shad is the most valuable river fish of the Atlantic Coast, and next to the Chinook salmon, the most important species inhabiting the fresh waters of North America. Among the economic fishes of the United States only the cod and the Chinook salmon exceed it in value."

Nowadays one has to search long and hard to find shad, or even shad roe, available in fish markets, even in season. Yet the return of the shad in major rivers following the environmental clean-up and construction of fishways is an ecological miracle. All those bones protect it! Not so in India. In the Calcutta fish markets it is widely available and fairly expensive. A favorite recipe, in her cookbook, *Bengali Cooking*, is provided by my Bengali wife, Manisha.

MANISHA'S MUSTARD HILSA

INGREDIENTS

1 pound of hilsa or shad, sliced into 1-inch steaks

1 tsp. turmeric

3 tsp. mustard powder

2 green chili peppers, cut into ½-inch pieces

1 tsp. black cumin seeds

1 tsp. salt

1 large onion, finely chopped

2 Tbsp. oil

Mix the mustard powder in 1 cup warm water. Rub the fish in turmeric and salt. Heat the oil, fry the cumin seeds quickly, then add the chopped onion and cook until translucent. Add the fish and brown both sides for about a minute. Add the mustard liquid , cover the pan, and simmer until done, when the fish is just opaque and flakes easily off the bones, which are many.

This dish is delectable, and enhanced by a mild beer or shandy. A rice pilau goes nicely with it.

A fascinating diversion from fishing is to visit the Holyoke Power Station and to see the method of transporting the upstream migrants. At the junction of the dam base and the power station building is a walled pool with a narrow entrance into the river. The shad and other anadromous fishes eventually find their way upcurrent into the pool where they enter a cage that is periodically lifted thirty feet by cables, to discharge into a water passage that communicates with the river above the dam. They are thus transported over the dam by elevator.

Spectators can see the fish through an underwater viewing window along one wall of the passage. Here, staff from the U.S. Fish and Wildlife Service record the numbers of shad and others that make the ride. Earnest young guides shepherd the spectators and provide them with useful or other information.

The shad count when the fishway was built in 1955 came to only 4,889. The annual migration grew steadily and exceeded 100,000 by 1975. In contrast, the return of the salmon has been sparse and erratic. Only 368 were counted in 1992.

Thus, thanks to cleaner rivers and removal of barriers, the "poor man's salmon" has staged a dramatic comeback in the past several decades. Not so the salmon. This may be due to the decimation of salmon in their traditional feeding grounds near Greenland. The buying up of netting licenses and the improved economics of salmon farming may eventually reduce the incentive for netting of wild salmon. I hope that the salmon will return to our American rivers. But in the meantime I will enjoy fishing for shad on the Connecticut each spring in jovial companionship with fellow anglers.

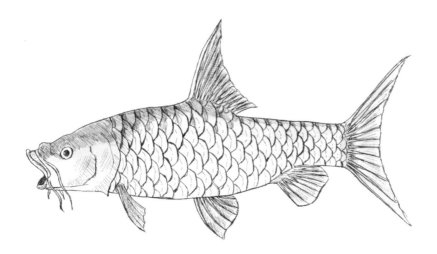

CHAPTER 13

The Elusive Mahseer

"There he met the mahseer of the Poonch beside whom the tarpon is as a herring and he who lands him can say he is a fisherman."

(from Rudyard Kipling's 'The Brushwood Boy')

In my long love affair with India and in reading about its wildlife, the name of this legendary gamefish kept appearing. But in the nineteen-fifties I was more a tourist, a viewer of temples and towns; in the sixties I was preoccupied with medical matters in India, and in the seventies the fish was said to have become extinct—a victim of dams and dynamite. But some Anglo-Saxon piscatorial pioneers, Bob Howitt, Andrew and Martin Clark, and Paul Boote, "rediscovered" the mahseer in the late seventies, at least for western sport fishermen. Glowing reports and dramatic pictures of giant fish restimulated my interest and, in the winter of 1992, I was able to get away from the customary visits to in-laws, hospitals, and medical conferences to try for the mahseer.

HER FACE FLUSHED WITH EXCITEMENT, the lady from Liverpool showed us her lacerated right index finger and exclaimed, "'E bluddy near tore it off!"

Her finger had experienced the power of the mighty mahseer stripping line from her heavy casting reel.

The mahseer, or *Barbus (Cyprinus) tor*, belongs to the Family *Cyprinidae*, which includes minnows, tenches, carp and goldfish, and Genus Tor. It once populated all the colder fast flowing rivers of India. It was the favorite game-fish, the "Indian salmon," of British sportsmen in the prime of the Empire.

In the forty-five years of my acquaintance with India, I have seen a doubling of the population and known changes in governmental priorities, both of which have resulted in a major destruction of India's wilderness and its once prolific wild life. All nine varieties of *Barbus tor* are now listed among the twenty-five most endangered fish species in India.

But there have been positive responses to this crisis in the last decade or so. Aware of the ecological crisis confronting mahseer as well as other wild fauna in India, wild life associations, philanthropic societies, and governmental agencies have taken measures to reverse this tragedy. I had the chance to participate in some of those efforts.

The word 'mahseer' probably comes from the Sanskrit 'Maha Shira' (big head). These often gigantic fish certainly have big heads. They are related to barbels and carps, of which many varieties exist in the Indian subcontinent. But there the resemblance ends, for they are piscine pugilists, not placid inhabitants of lakes and ponds.

One of the largest, *Barbus tor Mussulah*, weighing as much as 200 pounds, dwells in the river Cauvery (Kaveri in Indian geographical terminology) and its tributaries.

I have often seen the Cauvery, largest river of southern India. It arises in the mountains of Coorg in the western part of Karnataka, formerly part of the princely state of Mysore, traverses the Deccan Plateau, and empties into the Bay of Bengal through the delta of Tanjore (*see map*). Indian newspapers often report the bitter dispute between the Karnataka and Tamil Nadu States over the rights to the Cauvery's water. Tamil Nadu receives only the dregs during the rice planting season in the spring.

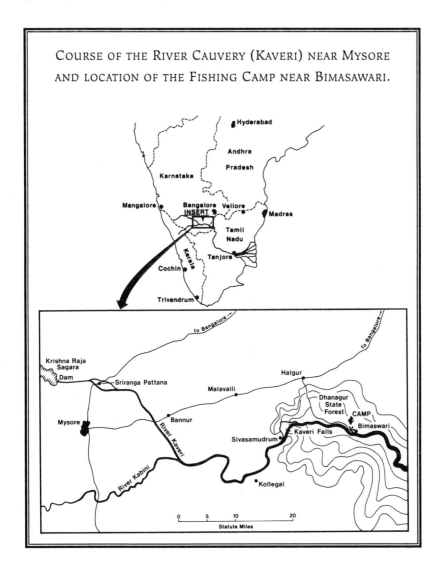

COURSE OF THE RIVER CAUVERY (KAVERI) NEAR MYSORE AND LOCATION OF THE FISHING CAMP NEAR BIMASAWARI.

I discovered that the Wild Life Association of Southern India (WASI) had formed a fishing preserve of a seventeen kilometer stretch of the river below the Cauvery Falls near Sivasamudram. Forest guards protect the area against the former widespread poaching. My interest focussed on this area and I resolved to support the program and to fish the Cauvery.

In preparation for pursuing a totally new and strange fish, I was fortunate to find a copy of the classic work, *The Rod in India*, written by Henry S. Thomas of the Madras Civil Service in 1873. In his survey of angling techniques, Thomas stated that fly-fishing for big mahseer is generally fruitless, successful only in clear and relatively shallow northern streams where the smaller mahseer reside. He believed that large spoons, or better, Ragi (a coarse grain) dough bait, were the only methods for the large mahseer of the Cauvery.

However, with the modern developments in fly-fishing such as fast-sinking lines, shooting tapers, and salt-water flies for related fish such as tarpon, I felt that hooking a large Cauvery mahseer on fly would be an exciting challenge—a long-shot perhaps, but a worthwhile adventure. It turned out, however, even after over one hundred years, that Mr. Thomas was right.

An opportunity came to visit South India again, after participating in a medical meeting in South Canara. The last leg of the trip from Boston to the Cauvery included a stop in Mysore City.

I had read about the famous Mysore taxidermists and sportsmen, the Van Ingen brothers, in an account by Clive Gammon (*I Know a Good Place*, David Godine, Boston, 1989) and arranged to visit them. They had a large tract on the outskirts of Mysore. I was greeted by a pleasant white-haired man in white bush shirt and khaki trousers. He introduced himself as Joubert Van Ingen.

"Would you like a drink?" His bright, enquiring eyes asked the question as much as his voice. "Gladly." And he led me to a verandah where another elderly man, de Wet Van Ingen, sat. Joubert was eighty-nine and de Wet, older, was nearly blind due to glaucoma. Both showed the ravages of a lifetime of tropical sun exposure to the skin but retained a vitality and alertness of much younger men.

Joubert Van Ingen brought in a bottle of English gin and a carafe of water (no ice) and served us. This was their prelunch cocktail and I dared not tarry long. After explaining my visit and my goals on the Cauvery, I asked about their history.

Joubert narrated. Their lives had been spent in India along with hunting trips to Africa. The brothers were sons of Eugen van Ingen, the founder of the taxidermy business in Mysore, in the 1920's, probably the largest and most famous in the world. They became, naturally, dedicated hunters and fishermen. The world record mahseer of 120 pounds was landed by de Wet Van Ingen in 1946 on the upper reaches of the Kabini River, a tributary of the Cauvery. This monster was mounted in their taxidermy shed.

From floor to ceiling in their spacious old-time bungalow were mounted dozens of stuffed heads, from tiger to antelope and even a gigantic mahseer head.

Joubert agreed with the prevailing notion that the Carnatic mahseer were mainly caught on bait, preferably "Ragi" doughballs. The mahseer were predatory omnivorous fish, feeding on everything from smaller fish and crustaceans to seeds and fruit—typical carp food. Large spoons were effective on occasion, however, and thus I hoped that one of my salt-water flies might work. Certainly others had written about fly-fishing with success for northern mahseer. I had a first-hand account about a twenty-eight pounder caught on fly by the adventurous Englishwoman, Lilla Rowcliffe, on the Ramganga in Corbett National Park located in the Kumaon foothills of the Himalayas.

My resolve in bringing a fly-fishing outfit equipped with fast sink shooting taper was strengthened. I would remain a "purist."

At dawn the following morning I embarked in an Ambassador

automobile, the durable Indian version of the 1954 Morris Minor, on a delightfully scenic ride over atrocious roads to the Cauvery. The scene of the Indian countryside as always was fascinating; the soft rosy morning, the convoluted distant hills, the wonderfully gnarled banyans and mangoes, the plowing and planting, the birds. As the morning progressed, the road filled with pedestrians, bicycles, ox-carts, and all types of motor vehicles ranging from motorcycles to lorries. There is a ballet with its own rhythm of Brownian motion (where no particle touches another) on Indian roads. Our car weaved an elegant pattern through the assorted moving obstacles, with each imperceptibly moving the centimeter or so from the point of expected impact.

The driver stopped for coffee in Bannur town. The market was just awakening to business. Shutters were raised, fires started, and stalls opened. The coffee was prepared by a sleepy attendant who poured boiling buffalo milk over a concentrated decoction of dark roasted beans, then added jaggery (unrefined cane sugar). He rapidly mixed and simultaneously cooled the mixture by dextrously pouring nearly a yard–long thin stream of coffee from one cup to the other. It was excellent.

The journey proceeded, and soon a range of hills loomed up ever closer. Using a U.S. Army topographic map (The U.S. military have mapped nearly the entire world) with scale of 1:250,000, I identified them as the Dhanagur Hills flanking the Cauvery River basin.

After passing Malavalli village we reached Halgur and turned off to the right on an unpaved, incredibly rutted, pot-holed road flanked by scenes of rice planting, plowing, threshing, and winnowing.

The surrounding landscape became more desolate and unpopulated as we proceeded. The road worsened, and then, at the end of the plateau, we saw the Cauvery valley stretched out below. The river, through the now-shimmering haze of late morning, was a gleaming silver band dividing green masses of forest.

We descended quickly, nearly 1000 feet, feeling a perceptible rise of temperature from the pleasant coolness of the Mysore plateau to distinct but not uncomfortable heat. The Cauvery basin leads eventually to the river's outlet near Tanjore, 200 miles southeast on the Coromandel coast.

Plunging down to the valley floor, the remarkably resilient Ambassador then forded several small streams and dry gulleys, and, sixteen kilometers from Halgur, finally reached our goal, a cluster of tents on the river's bank.

The first human scene was a file of khaki-uniformed men with rifles slung over their shoulders amidst which marched a forlorn-looking dhoti-clad man. This event I later found was frequent, the arrest of poachers by forest guards.

We reached the camp, and the smiling manager, Kumar, emerged to greet me, offer coffee, and give the usual introduction to the camp routine. I was the only guest.

It was eleven A.M., too late for morning fishing. The next event would be lunch. I explored the campsite, and settled into my tent, which was well furnished with two cots, a table, flashlight and candles, and an adjoining concrete block bath house with western-style commode, sink, and shower.

I put on swim trunks, walked down to the river, and sank contentedly into the 70-degree water, letting the swift current wash away the dust of the journey.

I had bought some bananas, apples, and oranges in Halgur, not being sure of the availability of fresh fruit at the camp. They were in a sack that I placed in the coolest place just outside the tent. On my return the sack was empty; I was nonplussed and angry, wondering how thievery could occur in this pastoral setting. Only later did I realize what had really happened, something about India that I had forgotten—yes, thievery, but by the quiet, watchful monkeys, sitting in the surrounding trees, waiting for opportunities.

The river was large, perhaps the size of the Connecticut River. At low water in February, however, many rocks, small and large rapids, pools and quiet stretches, characterised the conditions. A good bit was wadeable but in no place was it fordable. Large banyan and wild mango trees flanked the shoreline, reeds and shrubs dotted the sandy beaches. The latter showed marks of basking gharial, the Indian crocodile,' which had slipped into the water before my approach. The water was moderately turbid, with a visibility of about three feet. I saw occasional rises, but there were no visible insects or hatches. None of the guides could explain to what the fish, the Carnatic carp, were rising.

Luncheon was served in an open central dining area covered by a conical galvanized-steel roof. The food was good Indian fare—chappatis, mutton curry, vegetables, rice, pappads, cucumber and tomato salad, a variety of condiments, and a sweet.

As we were eating, a car pulled in and a second guest appeared, complete with heavy tackle that was in sharp contrast to my light fly-fishing equipment.

We quickly became acquainted over lunch. Jim was assigned to the U.S. Embassy in New Delhi. He was a dedicated angler whose quest had taken him around the world in search of the biggest and rarest fish. He had pursued blue marlin, yellowfin tuna, giant sturgeon, tarpon, Nile perch, and other trophy fish. He represented to me a different breed of fisherman, the specimen and trophy angler. The method of capture was generally secondary to the goal.

I found Jim a pleasant, gregarious new companion and we enjoyed discussing the history of the mahseer and the early Anglo-Indian descriptions of fishing in India. He had done his homework and knew the taxonomy and natural history of this, the greatest of Indian freshwater gamefish.

After a short siesta while the temperature rose well into the nineties, the guides came to our respective tents, and roused us. A jeep was waiting, our gear was loaded, and we were driven about a kilometer upstream to the "Temple Pool," named for the ruins of a Hindu shrine in the hills above a large lake-like pool of the Cauvery.

Our guides now brought out the expected bait—for bait was *de rigeur* for big mahseer on the Cauvery. It consisted of a paste or dough made of Ragi flour, a common grain in India, mixed with a variety of condiments. The dough is molded into a firm ball on the large 2/0 treble hook and is cast, without need of additional weight, far out into the pool. My American friend cast repeatedly but was able to hook only some small mahseer. Their scales were large and iridescent with subtle shades of gold, the fins were prominent and rakish, and the mouths powerful. Considering the heavy tackle, they were good fighters but did not leap, but rather, stubbornly, used their flat bodies and fins for leverage, much like the American shad. The mahseer were carefully returned to the river because a strict catch-and-release policy prevailed in the entire protected length of the Cauvery.

I moved on with my guide, Venkatesh, to the rapids above the pool where I indulged myself with the ethereal pursuit of fly-casting. But never a take, despite careful probing of the depths with the fast sinking line, even including a lead core leader section. But it was enjoyable to wade through the rapids, searching for the elusive *Barbus*. The sunset was a gorgeous array of pinks and oranges fading into the short twilight of fuchsia and madder.

Next morning, after coffee at sunrise, Jim and I with our guides Joseph and Venkatesh embarked in a coracle for the Camp Pool. The Indian coracle, certainly one of the most ancient boat designs, is a circular concave tub made of interlacing strips of bamboo, covered with buffalo skin, and more or less waterproofed with tar. Surprisingly four persons can fit into it along with paraphernalia, and it moves rather well, even up rapids, with one man paddling.

The fishing continued to be poor with only smallish mahseer, Carnatic carp, and catfish caught on bait, and nothing on nymph or streamer. This would be the pattern for the remaining days of angling. The water was fresh and warm, the wading pleasant in shorts and wading shoes, and the surrounding wooded hills imparted a sense of peace and beauty.

During the following days two more fishing parties arrived and they soon became of more interest to me than the fishing. The first to arrive was a middle-aged couple from Liverpool.

We met at dinner and it took me a while to understand the thick Liverpudlian. I found them engaging and cheerful with, again, great enthusiasm for hooking "the big one."

Considerable publicity had been generated in British fishing circles about mahseer through magazine articles by Paul Boote and John Wilson, both fishing journalists, as well as through an excellent and dramatic video by Paul Boote on spinning for mahseer in a tributary of the Ganges.

Our Liverpool couple came well outfitted with heavy spinning and casting gear. My new companions were from a large fraternity of anglers in Britain who fished for what is referred to as coarse fish, as distinguished from regal fish such as salmon and trout. Coarse anglers have a fully developed fishing subculture to support their activities with clubs, magazines, equipment, and jargon all targeted to their needs. They have developed elaborate techniques and display remarkable patience in their pursuit of prize specimen fish.

The enthusiasm of the Liverpool couple paled in comparison, however, to that of the last arrival, a gregarious young cockney. I soon learned more about tench, roach, loach, perch, asp, rudd, chubb, gudgeon, and sturgeon than I cared to know. An exceptional enthusiast, he worked as a roofer in London six days a week, forty-eight or fifty weeks of the year, to save for a holiday exclusively devoted to fishing, no matter the cost. There was only one goal in coming to India, as with the Liverpool couple, and that was to fish for the mahseer. The sights and culture of India were only of passing interest. He brought with him the appropriate gear, but in addition an item that exemplified the high technology of coarse fishing—an electronic bite detector! He proudly demonstrated this device which emitted an audio and visual signal upon the slightest movement of the line. Certainly useful for night-fishing!

We were now divided into three fishing parties—Jim and I, the Liverpool couple, and the young cockney. In the morning and evening shifts we fished, in rotation, the Temple, Tiger, Camp, and Balumudu pools. These were all deep, large masses of water divided by rapids which I invariably fished. Monkeys sat watching silently on the river bank. They doubtless were puzzled by the strange antics of this pale stranger. My young guide fished with a casting rod and when there were signs of action, would cry "Sah, fish going nibble, nibble!" I would abandon the fruitless fly-fishing for a moment to take the rod and thus feel the mild excitement of hooking a small mahseer, Carnatic carp, or catfish.

I soon realized that my quixotic quest would probably be fruitless and concentrated more upon observing the landscape, waterscape, the plant and animal life, and my fellow man.

In the afternoons Venkatesh took a coracle upstream and we floated the rapids, shallows, riffles, and pools—excellent fly-fishing water. Occasional noisy rises broke the afternoon stillness. Under the overhanging wild mangoes, flurries of rises seemed related to the movements of monkey families above. I recalled my conversation with Lilla Rowcliffe when she described her success in fly-fishing the Cauvery underneath the monkeys. She attributed the rises to carp feeding on monkey droppings and acquired the camp title of the "monkey-shit lady"! I watched long and hard for evidence of this but could not verify her observations. The rises were to some smaller, imperceptible source, perhaps insects dislodged by the movement of the monkeys.

Following Lilla Rowcliffe's advice, in any case, I tied on dark brownish floating flies ranging from muddlers to ants and finally solved, I am confident, the mystery. The fish avidly took various terrestrial patterns such as grasshoppers and beetles. As the monkeys scampered through the branches, they dislodged insects that fell down to the waiting Carnatic carp. They were hard fighters and provided splendid sport with a light fly-fishing outfit.

The big mahseer fishing, however, was poor, which was, as admitted by Kumar, due to the exceptionally low water conditions caused by upstream diversion and damming in Karnataka. This was the high season for planting of paddy, and, at the same time, the driest time of the year. No wonder that the Tamils objected in the courts and on the streets to the strangulation of their lifeline to the Tanjore delta.

Everyone in camp became increasingly frustrated with the failure to hook a large mahseer, so one evening at dinner, the young technologist proposed a try at night fishing. The logic was sound: this was a fine opportunity to put his electronic bite detector to the test.

A conference was called with Kumar and the three guides. There was much shaking of heads by the guides, who saw their sleep interfered with, but were also concerned about the leopard in our vicinity that had so far taken several goats in the past week—who knows what may be next! The paying guests' wishes prevailed, however, and that night they embarked at midnight for a try at the Temple pool.

I slept soundly. The next morning at breakfast there was a glum and sleepy group of night-owls. No fish, no leopards, nothing at all had stirred their blood in the dark.

It began to appear that the enthusiastic anticipation of all of us for a large mahseer was doomed. This was aggravated by reading the camp guest-book where joyous anglers from Britain, Germany and Scandinavia described the heart-stopping experiences of hooking and releasing mahseer of up to seventy-five pounds. And this only about one month or so ago!

All was not to be in vain, however. As we gathered at lunch, the Liverpool couple came in on the jeep in a state of high excitement.

The wife, ironically the only non-dedicated angler among us, had managed to hook (and lose) what seemed to be a substantial mahseer. We all examined her index finger, scorched by the reel spool as the fish took off fifty yards or so of thirty pound test before she knew what was happening. Then—too late—with the help of the guide, she vainly tried to set the hook.

At least it was exciting; the story was endlessly recounted, with examination and cross–examination of all the details. All had the unspoken feeling of, "If only it could have been me!" But the brush with success raised the spirits and hopes of the others. I bade farewell to an invigorated group of anglers and friends, and embarked on the car journey to Bangalore, carrying with me a broken nine-weight fly-rod, broken not on a fish, but on a snag!

According to Kipling's criterion I was not yet a fisherman.

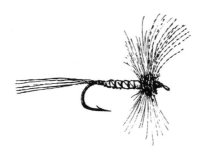

CHAPTER 14

Nordic Pilgrimage

*It was to be a roots-seeking journey. When in Scandinavia I
feel a beautiful resonance inside. Usually, that is. For example,
there is the culture shock of seeing roaring drunk Swedes on the
duty-free ferries between Denmark and Sweden, and Finns in the
same state on the Finland-Sweden ferries. There is no earthly paradise. In any case, I wanted to visit near and distant relatives, see
battlegrounds where ancestors fought and fell—usually against
the Russian enemy of old—and pay respects to our dead in graveyards throughout Sweden and Finland. But also to fish. The opportunity came in 1991.*

T HROUGH A SWEDISH RV MAGAZINE I negotiated a one-month
lease on a camper. Correspondence with numerous relatives
insured an occasional haven, opportunity to meet, and a hot bath.
The route included good fishing territory.

It finally happened in September. From Copenhagen's Kastrup air-

SCANDINAVIA AND FINLAND, SHOWING ROUTE.

port, by ferry to Malmö, and by train, I reached Lund in southern Sweden in a few hours and found the well-equipped Ritmo camper ready and waiting. With characteristic Swedish thoroughness the young owner indoctrinated me about the stove, refrigerator, heater, toilet, and engine. Within an hour I was on the road experiencing a heady feeling of freedom, like taking off on a long voyage—which it was.

The first stop was the quiet, old churchyard in Kristianstad where my parents and grandparents rest. The heady feeling was replaced by something closer to the heart. Images from decades past, like an old movie, rushed by as I looked down upon the place where I, and my wife, will also rest. I sought out the churchyard caretaker to give instructions on planting more of my favorite *Vinca alba*.

That evening I reached the town of Mörrum. I had heard that here was one of the finest salmon and sea trout fisheries in Scandinavia. The Mörrum River or Å (yes, one letter, å, means a river in Swedish) measured only fifteen kilometers or so in length on my map. It seemed to be just one of numerous smaller to larger streams draining the large glacial terrain of lakes, swamps, and bogs of southern Sweden into the Baltic Sea near Karlshamn on the southern coast. But the Mörrum is unique, I read, for being a valuable and prolific salmon fishery known since the Middle Ages. It is now a well-controlled, state-run fishery for sport anglers. It is not cheap to fish: depending on the season, a day ticket can cost $100. But that still cannot compare with fisheries of similar quality in Norway, such as the Alta, where an international fishing elite has pushed the prices sky-high, much to the satisfaction of the riparian owners.

The next morning I checked in at the small office and museum by the river. The Mörrum was a beautiful stream with all the attractive characteristics of a salmonid river—small waterfalls, deep pools, rapids, quiet shallows, and a rock and gravel bottom.

It was not in a wilderness, however. The paths were manicured, and benches sat along the streamside at regularly spaced intervals. Signs indicated the numbered pools.

I enquired at the office and was lucky enough to get a beat for the following day. September was the high season for sea-run browns that can reach thirty pounds in weight, and bookings are generally filled for weeks in advance.

The beats are assigned at random by computer; some pools for fly-fishing only, some for spinning, and the rest for both. In all, there are thirty-two pools or stretches that are assigned for morning or afternoon beats. Thus each angler has complete privacy to his assigned beats, a welcome change from some public fishing hotspots, but at a price.

After a good night's rest in the camper and a hearty breakfast, I assembled my gear and walked down to the river. My first sight was of a vigorous battle between a fish and a young spin-fisherman in jeans and t-shirt. He finally landed it, a fresh fifteen pound sea-run brown trout, and carried it to the mandatory weighing-in scales and registered the catch in the logbook.

In another pool I saw a determined looking fly-fisherman, dressed to the nines in a color-coordinated outfit. I later learned to recognize the well-turned out anglers as Swiss, French, or Germans; the rest, Swedes and others, were more casual in dress as well as in personality.

After fly fishing some assigned pools without any action, I stretched out on a sunny rock and had lunch—home-made sandwiches and good Swedish beer. With one hand I held the rod, allowing a black marabou streamer to swim in the downstream pool. After a time I was surprised to have the streamer snag on a rock, a rock that I had not thought was there. I pulled, and felt an immobile resistance. The rod was my six-weight, four-piece travel rod with a sink tip line and a six-pound-test leader tippet. I gingerly tried to unsnag the line by giving slack. Amazingly, the rock moved upstream.

Gradually, in a postprandial daze, I realized that I was on to a big fish, bigger than would be normally handled with my gear. It was downstream and I wore no waders, having light-heartedly assumed that a one-day experience on this famous stream would be a reconnaissance, not a serious fishing quest.

I immediately devised a strategy—apply maximum side pressure to move him out of the main current, give no quarter, and try to beach him, since I had no net or gaff. The rod bent critically as I gingerly clambered down off the rock into the shallows. The fight was lengthy; the fish was dour and stubborn, moving heavily back into the pool at the slightest release of pressure. A group of anglers and spectators lined up on the opposite bank to watch the battle. I gradually worked the monster back from the pool and for the first time saw his outline in the shallow water. To me he was frighteningly large. From his behavior he was a sea-run brown. A salmon would have leaped.

I backed slowly up to the shore and began to relax, although still worrying about the final landing. Luckily (I thought at the moment!) a fellow angler came to the rescue with a huge landing net. As he reached out the net the moment of truth came. With one heave the fish was off. He turned and swam slowly in a rather dignified way back to the pool with my fly in his mouth.

Sadly, the gaggle of onlookers dispersed. I looked at the end of the leader, which made me even sadder. It had not broken; the poorly tied knot had unravelled. This is known as learning a lesson the hard way.

The brown was at least ten kilos (twenty-two pounds) according to my erstwhile savior.

I left the Mörrum with bittersweet memories, resolving to return someday with proper equipment and carefully tied-on tackle.

My path headed northward, through the heart of Sweden, Dalecarlia. September was a cool month with occasional rain. Forests and lakes replaced the rolling hills and grain fields of southern Sweden. As I camped along the way, there were opportunities for foraging expeditions. Mushrooms, blueberries, lingonberries, and blackberries were abundant. I gleaned potatoes from nearby freshly harvested fields and became nearly self-sufficient with the trout caught in the small to large streams flowing eastward from the Norwegian fells and emptying into the Baltic Sea.

The camping was interspersed with visits to wonderfully hospitable relations along the way. Generally, the first gesture of hospitality is to partake in sauna (bastu in Swedish). This rite, repeated many times during my trip, has an almost religious significance to Scandinavians and Finns. The sauna is often a separate small log cabin consisting of two rooms—the sauna bath with woodburning stove and benches, and the outer room with one or more beds or cots for resting. The sauna is usually located on the shore of a lake or stream, important for the rapid cold immersion which shocks the system and must do something to the body's internal endorfin secretion, because I have rarely felt so good, at such peace with myself and everything around me, as following a good sauna.

The sauna is a social ritual as well. No pretences are possible when, totally naked, one communicates with another. The *persona* (from the Latin *per/sonare*, to speak through, i.e. through the mask of the Greek theater) is left outside. The Nordic social formality, often considered a coldness by others, nearly literally melts away.

Following the sauna, a traditional meal is served. The *smörgåsbord* in Scandinavia is nowadays much more Spartan than previously. However the basic dishes include herring in at least three different pickled varieties, small boiled potatoes, other fish dishes such as eel and anchovies, hardtack, bread, butter, and cheese. A salad of sliced cucumber in a watery dill or parsley vinaigrette is a suitable counterfoil for all the salty fish dishes. Gravlax (see chapter on Alaska) can be an added luxury but may also be a main dish.

All this is accompanied by the traditional *snaps*, or akvavit, a distilled spirit from fermented potatoes and grain, flavored with anise, caraway, fennel and cumin (see Chapter 1).

Following the combination of a sauna and such a meal, no guest is expected to stay up very long. An early bedtime or siesta is quite in order. Needless to say, I very much enjoyed these visits. And my extended family grew and grew in variety—schoolteachers, farmers, engineers, scientists, and poets.

I drove north through the province of Jämtland. The weather turned colder and it snowed. The countryside was now a forested wilderness dotted by small farms and tiny villages. I nearly collided with a moose that wandered across the road at dusk. I changed the goal of reaching Lappland, because of the worsening weather, and turned east toward the Gulf of Bothnia. Camping stops were always by the shores of promising trout and grayling streams. The only tedious feature was the need to buy a fishing permit for each stop.

Sweden, like all European countries, has antique fishing regulations, based upon historical riparian property rights. These rights, over 2000 of them, have been handed down or sold, often to regional fishing clubs or to tackle shop owners. The prospective angler must find the owner or a representative in order to buy a permit. Luckily, an annual guidebook covering the whole country gives details on buying permits (*Svenska Fiskevatten*). For the travelling tourist without a knowledge of Swedish, though, the situation is difficult, and he is probably better off getting information from a major tackle shop in a large city where English is better known.

In one example I camped on the banks of the Gim in Jämtland. This "å" is a "western"-looking river with all the characteristics needed for good fly-fishing water. Like so many rivers in the North, the Gim has mementos of past logging practice: large breastworks of boulders along the shores designed to prevent log jams; huge iron rings drilled into rocks for harnessing log piles. Logging practises have changed, leaving the rivers free for fishermen.

Outside of these features, the stream has the necessary rapids, pools, and shallows for wading to reach the holding spots.

This stream is known for its grayling, a fish that I had long sought. With information from the tackle shop proprieter (and permit issuer) I set out to capture this salmonid with the thyme-like odor (*Thymallus arcticus*).

The conditions were, unfortunately, unfavorable. A cold north wind blew down the stream and I spotted no rises or insects. I tried upstream nymphing which yielded a brace of nine-inch browns, adequate for supper. My fruitless quest for grayling was to continue until I reached Alaska.

The weather worsened and I detoured through Umeå on the coast of the northern Gulf of Bothnia, via ferry to the Finnish town of Jacobstad. The inhabitants of the coastal regions of Finland are often Swedish speaking. Here are concentrated my Finnish relations. Fewer than eight percent of all Finns use Swedish as their main language. They are a declining minority. Why is Swedish spoken at all in Finland?

I have learned that during the nearly four centuries of Swedish rule (from the 1400's to 1809), Swedish was the language of education, literature, and law in Finland. Finnish is a totally different language that is related to Estonian, Hungarian, Turkish, and, some say, Korean. It was first transcribed as a written language in the seventeenth century. The original tribal inhabitants of the eastern Baltic shores included the Letts, Ests, and Finns. Their origins are from the Huns, somewhere in the huge land mass between the Orient and Europe. The Swedes, Danes, and Norwegians were Germanic tribes with very similar languages who today can be understood by each other.

For centuries the Baltic tribes were dominated by the Scandinavians. Later the Germans invaded Prussia, Lithuania, Latvia, and Estonia in the northern crusades of the thirteenth century led by the Order of Teutonic Knights. From these origins a German-speaking military aristocracy dominated the region for centuries. It was known for its ruthless rule over the conquered inhabitants who were forcibly converted to Christianity, by the sword.

This military hegemony was to play a large role in the armed expansion of Sweden in the seventeenth century as it provided officers and men for the armies of Gustavus Adolphus on to Charles XII.

That is the background to my Swedish-speaking, predominately

Finnish family with a German name.

I visited more relatives along the way, enjoyed saunas, meals, and good company. We toured the countryside, exploring churches, battlefields, and graveyards where ancestors prayed, fought, died, and were buried.

The Finns, Swedish-speaking or not, are less verbal than any other group of people that I have met. Their virtues of honesty, directness, and bravery more than make up for this hindrance of communication; but, as always, notable exceptions exist. One relative, in her seventies, is a non-stop talker with eight volumes of poetry and an active political career to her credit.

I turned inland to explore trout waters. Not much time was left. The journey would eventually culminate in Stockholm where an historic gathering of the Swedish and Finnish branches of the family was to take place.

The Tainionvirta is near Hartola in south central Finland. This, like many rivers in the country of 10,000 lakes, is a connection between lakes. There are occasional rapids where the fly-fisherman can best enjoy his sport.

I camped, bought the local permit plus the national license from the post office and was ready to go. Wading out in the rapids, I was greeted by a young Finnish angler. We found a common base of communication in English.

"You will find a big fish above the rapids," he said.

"How big?" I asked.

"Two kilos or more. He was rising, but I could not interest him with my fly."

"What fly are you using?"

"This one." He showed me a large elkhair muddler. I had seen some insect activity, but none to match the likes of that. The mayflies were small olives, resembling a size twelve Adams.

I thanked him for his help and moved upstream. Dusk was approaching and the stillness of the air brought out some large Finnish mosquitos. Presently I saw him.

In a pool just above the rapids, a dimple appeared on the mirror-smooth water. The dimple recurred at intervals of thirty seconds.

It is said that the larger the trout, the smaller the rise. If so, this could be a large trout. I was anxious to find out.

The rises were to spent spinners. I tied on the nearest imitation and picked a strategic position twenty feet below and to the right of the rise-form. I gingerly snaked out line with false casts and was able, for once, to place the fly approximately where I wanted it to land—two feet above and six inches to the right of the dimple pattern.

Many accounts of this ceremony, the Presentation of the Fly, record the frustrations and repeated attempts to lure the wise old trout with his figurative magnifying glass. It adds to the suspense and heightens the reader's vicarious pleasure when the climax (for there must be a climax, else why describe the foreplay?) is reached. Suspense, however, cannot be further drawn out in my case.

The fly floated down, the dimple reappeared, and the fly was no longer there! A gentle sideways abduction (not even saying "God save the Queen") and he was on. A lunker!

He headed straight up the pool, and I exerted maximum pressure on the three-pound test leader. He turned back into the rapids and I was in trouble, sliding and skipping downstream to stay below him. He was surely a brown, only revealing himself as I coaxed him toward the shallows.

With grunts of exertion I managed to beach him, to the admiration and possible envy of my Finnish acquaintance. The trout was bright, with startling red and black polka dots along his flanks—a very good five-pounder.

Then, to my new friend's amazement and groans, I released the noble animal. And I have felt good about it ever since.

I caught, however, more trout. They were pan-sized and the

Finnish landscape provided the potatoes, lingonberries and mushrooms. Which leads to the following recipe which is based upon available ingredients in the RV.

TROUT à la TAINIONVIRTA

INGREDIENTS

Trout, fresh and cleaned as described previously
1 cup wild mushrooms, ideally chantarelles
2 tsp. green ("Madagascar") peppers in brine
Oil
Salt to taste

PREPARATION

Briefly sauté the peppers in oil, add the mushrooms, sauté until just done, add the trout and sauté both sides, spooning the ingredients into the bellies. Add a little white wine at the end.

Serve with lingonberry preserve and fresh-dilled new potatoes. A very dry white wine, even a Muscadet, can go well with this. The spicy green peppers and the sweet-sour lingonberries give an intriguing interplay of tastes with the delicacy of the trout and the gaminess of the mushrooms.

The journey was near the end. I had embraced my kin, tasted the soil, absorbed the air and light of the lands of my forefathers. The roots were deep.

CHAPTER 15

Kings and a Grizzly on the Aniak

It's good to have friends, especially fishing friends. Although I am a loner and many of my expeditions have been solo, I was reluctant to tackle Alaska on my own—even though I had dreamed about that wilderness from childhood when I had absorbed Jack London's stories about the Far North like a sponge. Bob's telephone call, therefore, in early 1992, was like a voice from Heaven. A friendly bear of a man, he had been my preceptor in laboratory research at Stanford over thirty years before. I, in my turn, had taught him what little I knew about fly-fishing. We had fished and camped in the early days; then career led me away to the East and abroad. We had stayed in touch, however, and this trip, organized by him, was for his friends and I was glad to be counted among them.

I GAZED UP THE AISLE OF THE CHICAGO-ANCHORAGE 757 and seethed at the snail-like approach of the food cart. Something had gone akilter in the flight kitchen. We had waited two hours after the appetite-arousing cocktail service. Around me, passengers with pinched expressions also focussed on the busy, annoyingly cheerful attendants.

True hunger has been a rare experience. I felt distinctly testy and hostile and wondered if a hungry grizzly might feel the same. Would I meet one this time? The untameable, primitive, and dangerous *Ursus* symbolized for most the wildness of Alaska.

The eventual meal, no better and no worse than most, soothed the hostility and even allowed a certain jovial bantering between passengers and staff during the remaining five hours of flight.

The Anchorage region was wet and overcast. It reminded me of Norway—glacial coastline, deep green woods, and snowy mountains. The landing was smooth.

The taxi driver, following the usual pleasantries, asked me, "Did you hear about the bear killing?" I took a long breath, "No, tell me about it." The tale was quite gruesome. A young couple was vacationing in a lakeside cabin near Glenallen, some 200 miles northeast of Anchorage. A bear prowling on the porch awoke them. They tried to drive him off by shouts and banging of kitchen pans. Instead he became more aggressive, drove them back inside the cabin, and then, incredibly, broke through a window and drove them out. They sought refuge on the roof, drawing up a ladder after them. The bear refused to leave and continued his threatening behavior. Finally the husband made a dash for help.

He returned within a half-hour with armed neighbors, but they discovered the bear a few yards from the cabin devouring the woman. The animal was promptly dispatched with several bullets.

It was a young male, 150-pound cinnamon brown grizzly, thin but otherwise in perfect condition.

The *Anchorage Daily News* reported this story in a matter-of-fact way, noting almost in reproach that the couple had neglected to have any anti-bear devices such as bear repellant, firecrackers, or firearms. The motives for the attack were not clear, but the possibility of rabies was raised.

I read the details, appalled at the synchronicity with my feelings on the plane. Then, to surmount the story, there came another report on the evening news of a bear killing, this time a grizzly attack on an eight-year-old boy in King Cove on the Alaskan Peninsula.

What would come next? Bob had assured me that he had seen just one bear, at a distance, in all three trips to the fishing camp near Aniak.

The next morning we all assembled at the airport. It felt good to see friends and colleagues of many decades. The friendly banter and reminiscing foretold a congenial reunion.

My five companions varied in age from early fifties to over seventy. We knew each other, as old friends, as scientific colleagues, and now, as fishing comrades. The initial scientific and medical shoptalk gradually evaporated over the next several days, to be replaced by fish talk, gossip, and nostalgia.

Alan was a raconteur of stories, dirty and otherwise, whose jovial, hoarse-voiced manner masked a distinguished life in science. Ted, like me a good listener, was a novice to fishing. Although chairman of a large, distinguished medical school department, he easily became again a student. Les and Martin, both Englishmen and excellent scientists, balanced our raucous antics with a quiet, contemplative, and gentlemanly love of fishing, the heritage of the English chalkstream.

Our great expectation was to see and catch the mighty Pacific king or Chinook salmon (*Oncorhynchus tshawytscha*). But other salmonids and char of Alaska were on our wish list: chum salmon (*Oncor. keta*), Humpy (*Oncor. gorbuscha*), rainbow trout (*Oncor. mykiss*), Arctic char (*Salvelinus alpinus*), and grayling (*Thymallus arcticus*). We were to catch all of these, sometimes on the same day.

The pilot of the 1900 Beech sixteen-seater turboprop pointed out landmarks as we flew over the snowy Alaska Range west of Anchorage. We six oldsters gawked and snapped picture after picture while the only other passengers, Inuit schoolgirls on their way home, giggled and gossiped in Yup'ic.

We continued over a trackless wilderness of forest, lakes, and rivers for nearly one and a half hours. It was the climax to my dream of finally seeing this, one of the remaining portions of our natural world.

The town of Aniak was a cluster of houses and a landing strip on the shore of the Kuskokwim River. The lodge owner, our host for the week, and his young guides and helpers, greeted us and loaded our luggage into a van. Soon we were at the riverside, transferring luggage into a powerboat for the final stage of the long trip.

The boat trip, which lasted an hour and a quarter, took us up the Aniak River to the lodge. The river is a branch of the Kuskokwim which parallels the Yukon just to the north. The Aniak flows due north and is flanked by the Kwethiuk and Halitna rivers. The Kuskokwim empties into Kuskokwim Bay on the Bering Sea at Bethel, just above the Aleutian chain.

The lodge was comprised of a group of raw wood frame buildings, raised four feet above ground on heavy beams. The main lodge had a large comfortable living and dining room with a large wood-burning stove, constantly stoked, even in July. The living quarters for the guests were located down a corridor. They were Spartan but clean, with comfortable bunks.

We were all anxious to get out on the river, and, despite swarms of evening mosquitos, several flyfished the river branch just by the lodge. The first arctic char, grayling, and rainbow of the trip were readily caught on fly and returned. The first flush of predatory excitement hit us and the conversation shifted continuously to the main

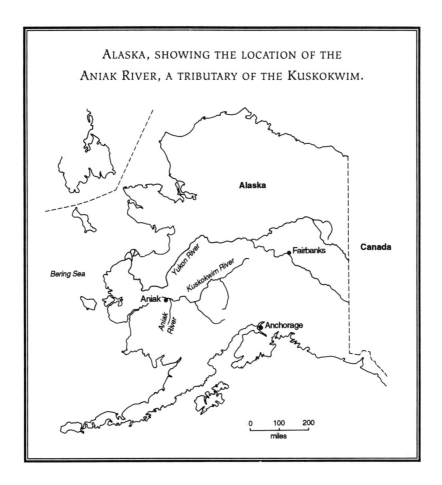

ALASKA, SHOWING THE LOCATION OF THE
ANIAK RIVER, A TRIBUTARY OF THE KUSKOKWIM.

prey, king salmon. The details of the spawning run, and the experience of the previous fishing party, whetted our anticipation.

After a late, sumptuous supper of steak, salmon, mashed potatoes
and vegetables, and some desultory story-telling, reminiscing, and
piscatological talk, we retired, although the arctic twilight persisted
until nearly midnight.

Early next morning before breakfast, several enthusiasts were
already down on the river. That bizarre, somewhat obscene fly called
the egg-sucking leach, was effective for all species, even for baby
grayling scarcely larger than the fly.

Breakfast, and all those that followed, was a he-man affair of eggs, bacon, fried fish, country-fried potatoes, home-baked bread, marmalade, and coffee. The cooking was excellent, and we arose from the table with sufficient calories to pursue the big Chinook to Timbuctoo.

Two powerboats were waiting with our host, Larry, at the helm of one. He was a burly man who combined the qualities of a frontiersman and an entrepreneur. Next to his seat was a holstered Colt .38 caliber revolver, our security blanket against bear attack. We left the dock and zoomed upstream, the powerful twin turbojet engines throwing up roostertails of wake. As we sped at thirty-five MPH, the river became more tortuous and narrow, with frequent rapids and narrow channels between all sorts of flood debris, log-jams, rocks, and islands. The boats snaked their way through these channels with surprising, and often hair-raising, agility.

Eventually we reached our first goal, a place we would later name "the honey hole." It was a deep pool behind a riffle that paralleled the main river. The water level was high and slightly off-color from recent rains. We could not spot fish under these conditions and were instructed where to fish. Almost immediately the spinning lures connected with a variety of species—chum salmon running up to ten pounds, Chinooks to twenty pounds, and arctic char to three pounds. I gasped with astonishment. It was a virtual aquarium of large fish. The magnificent Chinooks, now pink sided in early spawning colors, certainly earned their other sobriquet—"king." The chum, also disparagingly called "dog," was no mean fighter either. The battles raged on both sides of me. The English expression "to play" a fish seemed as out of place as the German and Swedish equivalent verb, "drill."

I slaved away with the nine-weight fly rod, trying a variety of sinking lines and flies without success. The goal was to find the river bottom and get a good, long drift of the fly, an outrageous pattern called

Alaskabou, a 2/0 hook festooned with hot pink and orange marabou feathers. My friends began to connect with purple Alaskabous and I switched, still without success. I was beginning to feel despair at the prospect of another skunking, as in my quest for big mahseer, when the powerful strike and prolonged throb of a heavy fish shook me out of my depression. It was a chum, a beautiful medium-sized salmon with a variegated brown-gray-cream skin. (Later, after the first flush of success, we were to regard these fish as superfluous, and an annoyance to hook, preferring the greater elusiveness, weight, and fighting qualities of the king).

Soon Bob, then others of our group, began to hook kings on fly while I watched with envy. I usually pride myself on having a disengaged attitude about catching fish—"the game's the thing!"—but could not avoid feeling some competitive emotions. Perhaps that is why I prefer to fish alone.

Was I trying too hard? Had my instinct for the chase atrophied? Was my relationship with myself awry? Did I need the counsel of a Zen master? After closing my eyes and meditating while up to the waist in the cold waters of the Aniak River, the revelation came.

What was I here for anyway? I reminded myself that it was not just to catch fish but to meet old friends and share the camaraderie of the hunt. It was less important, but nevertheless fulfilling, to sink a line into the unknown waters and experience the anticipation and then the adrenalin-surging surprise of making a connection with that invisible force from our primitive origins: to battle and then, hopefully, to surmount the atavistic urge and return the prey unharmed to his home.

Yes, fresh salmon was delicious and there was something special about eating one's catch. Luckily the State of Alaska (and our host) limited our "keepers" over the entire time to the equivalent of one day's limit, which ranged from zero rainbows to two kings and five chums.

No, I was not here just to catch fish. That realization somehow unblocked a creative force. My mind cleared, my natural instincts returned. I moved out into the river with the swift current tugging at the chest-high waders. This was my element—get in as deep as possible in proximity to the prey. No fancy distance casting (I am a mediocre caster); read the water and trust instinct and intuition.

There was a long smooth glide of the river at one edge of the riffle where hydrodynamic action surely had carved a long trench in the river bed. If kings behaved like steelhead, they might be lying there, snout to tail, in the sheltered current, ready to move upstream. I cast a purple and pink marabou streamer to the head of the glide and, by constantly mending the sink-tip nine-weight line upstream, achieved a satisfactory dead drift of the lure down the center of the glide. A barely perceptible twitch of the floating line induced me to strike and—voilà! a powerful tug answered my wrist flexion, and my prayer. There was a pause, then an explosion: twenty yards of line were stripped off the reel and a good dusky orange salmon leaped and changed direction, forcing me to rapidly retrieve. A battle of strength and wits followed. He (for that is what we found) headed for a sunken pile of driftwood necessitating applying maximum and precarious side pressure that barely succeeded in diverting him from the sanctuary that would certainly have saved him. I frantically worked on the drag control of the reel which had developed the unfortunate tendency to bind. I finally settled on setting a light drag and palming the reel (and later resolved, for big game fishing, to buy a really good reel with a smooth, reliable drag, after appreciating the exquisite smoothness of drag of a Vom Hofe reel that Alan had brought).

Finally my prey was brought to net—a fifteen-pound male Chinook—photographed, admired, and released. This rusty magnificent fish seemed also a symbol of Alaska, with its wild power and determination that shook up my softened, "civilized" psyche.

After this, things went better. I had gained confidence and more understanding of my prey, where he was and how he reacted. And, as before, there came the ineffable feeling of harmony between Self and Nature. Was this a religious experience? Was my church the river and host a fish?

The ensuing days melted into each other in a blur of activity. We spent the long days on the river exploring new holding places after the "honey hole" faded in popularity. The water level dropped rapidly and fishing became more difficult. Kings were harder to find. There was always good fishing activity however, and some anglers, notably Lester and Martin, seemed to have the golden touch.

Evenings at the lodge were spent in drinking, eating, and chatting with companions about what otherwise would be considered inconsequential. We did not need the trappings of Akademia or Aesculapius. Bob had brought a generous amount of fresh dill and mustard for the preparation of gravlax, also called gravad lax. Thanks to his Danish wife, Ingrid, he is an enthusiast for things Scandinavian. We selected a large filet from the day's catch and proceeded to cure it. There were many quzzical looks and snide remarks from our colleagues and the lodge crew. Who ever heard of eating raw salmon, except perhaps the Japanese?

Grav, of course, means grave. The salmon was buried under rocks in the ancient days to force out the water and oil slowly and help the curing process.

The next morning, Larry informed us, with some satisfaction, that there was a stench from the refrigerator. I wondered if we had made a mistake in the proportions or technique. I poured off the large amount of expressed aromatic salmon juice, added more curing mix and hoped for the best. That evening Bob and I took out the filet which now had the firm, translucent texture of proper gravlax and sliced it for canapés to be served during our cocktail hour. Bob made the mustard sauce, and we presented the completed gravlax to our skeptical friends. Slowly, then with increasing speed, the canapés disappeared with grunts of appreciation ringing in our ears. Our task was vindicated.

GRAVAD LAX

1. Select two fresh salmon filets, preferably from each side of the same fish. Wipe them (do not rinse) with a paper towel. One filet is also possible.

2. Rub in liberally on both sides of each filet a mixture of even parts of white sugar and kosher salt with finely chopped fresh dill and freshly ground black pepper to taste.

3. Place a well wrung, moist cloth or paper towel in a rectangular glass baking dish. Put the filets, skin side out, together so that they match as closely as possible. Place them on the cloth, fold the cloth over the top, and put a plastic foil-wrapped brick or other substantial weight on top and refrigerate 12 to 24 hours.

4. Remove and rinse out the cloth in hot, then cold water, wring it out, or change paper towels. Rub more of the curing mix onto the filets. Refrigerate again for 12 to 24 hours. The gravlax is then ready. It can keep, refrigerated, for 10 to 12 days.

SAUCE FOR GRAVAD LAX

(for eight persons)

INGREDIENTS

2 Tbsp. brown sugar

5-7 Tbsp. chopped fresh dill

3 Tbsp. prepared Dijon mustard

1 cup oil (preferably walnut or avocado, not olive)

2 Tbsp. rice vinegar

salt and pepper to taste

PREPARATION

1. Grind the dill into the sugar in a mortar. The sugar should become green.

2. Transfer to a bowl and stir in well the mustard and vinegar.

3. Add the oil, first drop by drop, then more steadily, continuously whipping with a fork or whisk. The mixture should be well homogenized, with a consistency of mayonnaise.

Gravlax is traditionally served sliced, with the mustard sauce, fresh dill for decoration, and toast or small boiled potatoes (again, with dill) as smörgåsbord. Plenty of freezer-cold akvavit (my favorites are the Swedish "O.P.Andersson," or the Danish Aalborg "Jubileum," but for homemade recipes see Chapter One) and light beer are essential lubricants. The singing of Nordic drinking songs will stimulate the digestion.

Fishing became more difficult as the water level dropped. Alan, who had the misfortune to have the airline misplace his luggage and rods, was, however, rewarded with the granddaddy of them all, a forty-pound king requiring a prolonged battle and downstream chase by boat.

My biggest salmon came on the third day. I had waded with a wading staff through a rather deep hole to the gravel bar nearly halfway across the river. A cast placed the purple Alaskabou at the head of a slick. I let the sink-tip line and short four-foot leader bring it down and, as it began to drag and swing around, a heavy fish struck and, as before, paused a moment before beginning its run. When it rolled on the surface I could see that it was really big and knew that I was in trouble halfway out in the river. While concentrating on playing the fish with my cranky reel and trying to keep it off-balance, I had to calculate the best way to get back to the shore without going head over heels in the deep current. Finally, gingerly probing a path with the wading staff in one hand and playing the monster with the other, I shuffled and pirouetted back through the pool with water lapping occasionally over the top of the chest waders. With great relief I reached shallower water and could finally concentrate on bringing in the king. After a prolonged battle, I eventually brought the giant to net. Larry gave me instructions on how to hold a large, struggling salmon for the mandatory photograph, but I could scarcely lift it with my arms and shoulders really aching from the battle. It was a thirty-pound female which I gladly released after reviving her in the current. Bob later wrote me to say that it was the most dramatic fish-catching of the trip—a compliment that I will always cherish.

Alan, my roommate, is certainly the most experienced fisherman (and storyteller) of our bunch of scruffy scoundrels. I was delighted when he gave fly-tying demonstrations to me and the others. The first demonstration was the creating of that oddity, the egg-sucking leach. Using fluorescent yarn for the egg, it turned out to be quite simple. For the rest of the flamboyant Alaskan lures such as Alaskabous, Popsicles, etc., the techniques were easy enough and one's imagination was the only limit on the variety of colors and patterns. Our experience, however, suggested that certain colors seemed to be preferred under particular conditions. Purple surely outclassed pink or orange for the big kings during our week on the river. The eggs and egg-sucking leaches were definitely best for rainbows, char, and even grayling. This probably reflected the ovo-cannibalism stimulated during spawning.

One of the young guides took me one afternoon by a smaller dory-like boat up one of the side streams of the Aniak. It was beautiful: crystal clear water, from burly rapids to quiet deep pools, gravel bottom, fallen tree trunks and driftwood log jams—all the conditions to delight a fly fisherman. I rigged the six-weight seven and a half-foot rod with a three pound test leader and began casting upstream. Casting an Adams into the riffle above a pool led to catching and releasing several grayling ranging from one to two pounds. They had beautiful, shimmery, greyish violet bodies and the characteristic sail-fish-like dorsal fin. I admired these lovely fish for a particular reason.

For years I had sought the elusive grayling. The first contact was in 1959 in Yellowstone. The small lake was dotted with rings from rising grayling. But that was in the dark ages of my fly fishing ability and I quickly flogged the grayling down into the depths. Later, in Switzerland, on the river Reuss flowing from the Vierwaldstättersee by Lucerne into the Rhine, I saw the telltale rises of grayling on a winter's day, light dimples in clusters at the tailwater of long pools. This time they were beyond reach of my light line. The third time was in northern Sweden on the Gimån, a wild, boulder strewn stream known for its grayling. But never a touch. Now I was in grayling paradise. Dry fly, wet fly—all worked, once I knew they were there.

One morning I fished the sidestream near the lodge with the light trout outfit. Beside the char and grayling there were known to be some big rainbows. Casting to the far bank at the head of a run, using the customary egg-sucking leach, I hooked and released a respectable eighteen-incher. Moving up, I heard and saw a huge splash, again near the far undercut bank, and quickly tied on the largest fly, a monstrous brownish-purple sculpin on a 2/0 hook. I cast so that it landed on the bank of the stream, then let it plop into the rapid, and was rewarded with a magnificent, awesome take. The large rainbow came nearly halfway out of the water. The carnivorous fish was evidently fond of lemmings, which the fly also imitated. It gave a spectacular display of aerial acrobatics. Eventually I was able to tail, measure, and release the gorgeously colorful fish. It was twenty-three inches long. The boldness of the colors was startling. I sensed that this magnificent fish, now so ubiquitous throughout the world, has his natural home here, where he can shine and glow as beautifully as his ancestors.

Every evening we assembled for drinks and vivid stories recounting the day's exploits. A great feeling of camaraderie prevailed. The Englishmen, Martin and Les, were our best fish-getters, Bob, the most determined (I do not understand how his casting arm lasted so long!), Ted, the most philosophical and accepting of all circumstances, Alan, with the worst luck (re luggage) but the biggest fish, and I—but this is my story.

Two further highpoints of the Aniak adventure were the Night of the Grizzly and the Affair of the Broken Rod.

The Night of the Grizzly

AFTER THE GUESTS RETIRED ON THE THIRD NIGHT, at about eleven, Larry awoke me and said that there was a bear prowling around the lodge. Would I like to see him. I had a very strange feeling. What was it? Déjà vu? With a certain fear but also excitement at confrontation with *Ursus horribilis*, I rapidly dressed and joined the others. The bear had circled the camp and was apparently headed for the river where salmon had been gutted and dressed earlier in the evening. In silence we crept down to the landing and took places for relative safety in one of the power boats near where the carcasses had been dumped. We patiently waited. Presently he appeared. In the Arctic twilight his pelt was a glowing, glossy, golden cinnamon. He was a beautiful young grizzly of perhaps 250 pounds. He began to chew on a salmon carcass. I was excited. He was about twenty feet from us. Stupidly, I stood up in the boat to get a clear shot, and took a flash picture. He reared, snorted, and (luckily) scampered into the brush with the fish. Larry shook his head at me and said, "You shouldn't have done that." I realized the danger of my action. The bear could have reached us in about six bounds. But he was a young, happy, salmon-fed grizzly. He did *not* feel the way I had felt on the Chicago–Anchorage flight.

The Affair of the Broken Rod

FOR ME, THE *PIÈCE DE RÉSISTANCE* CAME IN THE LAST FEW HOURS of the last day on the Aniak. The water was low and clear. Many chum salmon were splashing their way upstream. I rigged the nine and a half-foot for nine-weight four-piece travel rod which had been the staunch weapon for the large fish throughout the entire week. As I hooked a salmon and set the hook a trifle harder than usual, the rod simply snapped in two. The graphite fibers must somehow have become fatigued from the many battles.

I was dismayed, not only at the damage, but at the forced end of salmon fishing. My chagrin was increased when the guide pointed out a school of kings slowly entering the pool. By then, with the help of polarized glasses and the clear low-water conditions, we had all learned to spot king salmon. There they were! Long torpedo shapes, dusky orange-hued, in Indian file, hugging the bottom. What the heck! I still had intact my lightweight rod. Hadn't I nearly landed a twenty-two pound sea trout on the Mörrum in southern Sweden with the same rod? A carelessly tied-on fly had been my undoing.

I quickly rigged the seven-and-half-footer, tied on a six–pound test leader to the butt of the sink-tip line, and carefully, this time, tied on the favorite egg-sucking leach. I positioned myself strategically above and to the side of the line of dusky salmon. The casting distance into the pool was a respectable forty feet. With vigorous double-hauling the fly was placed approximately at the calculated spot, and it sank downstream toward the row of piscine torpedos. With heart in my throat, I saw a shape detach itself from the battle column and slowly, leisurely, rise to inspect and then engulf the bizarre lure.

I struck on sight—no snap this time—and it was on! The king stripped off the fly-line down to the backing as I cautiously but firmly palmed the dragless reel. Carefully playing the salmon, I eventually brought him to net. He was a fine fifteen-pounder, by no means a big king, but for me, in these circumstances, the biggest challenge faced during the entire trip.

The tiny Aniak airport building was filled with fishermen, coming and going. Our gang, bubbling with high spirits, boarded the plane for the return flight to Anchorage and home. We were tired and happy.

CHAPTER 16

Pisco Sours
and Patagonian Trout

I had experienced some of the wonders of the southern land masses of Africa and Australasia where populations of European trout and salmon and American rainbows and brookies had been introduced by intrepid piscatorial pioneers in the last century. I learned that the same happened in Chile and Argentina. And there was more. Joshua Slocum's description of sailing into the boulder infested "Milky Way of the sea . . . northwest of Cape Horn" throbs in my mind and sends shivers down my spine. The writings of Darwin, Theroux, and Chatwin also evoke in me the remoteness and wildness of Patagonia. I often recall W.H. Hudson's Idle Days in Patagonia. *His introspective image is of a remote, mostly gentle, but also brutal wilderness that sometimes tolerates Man. The compelling prose reminds me of Thoreau. Those two men could be carved from the same block of granite.*

Thus I came to explore a bit of Patagonia. This time, however, there was no professional excuse to visit—no, just pay up and enjoy. And I did, twice, in 1994 and 1995.

VOLCAN OSORNO IS A PERFECT CONE, snowcapped, a Patagonian Fujiyama. In the shadow of its 2661-meter peak runs the
Rio Petrohué, our goal. We drove past the huge, sparkling Lago Llan-
quihué, past small, neat homesteads. The view of the lake and the
volcano was picture postcard perfect. Manisha was enchanted. We
stopped at the Vyhmeister *estancia* for *Küchen* and coffee. Blond-
headed children named Hans, Peter, and Gretchen played in the
sunshine and chattered in Spanish. A sad looking, disabled condor
sat on a perch looking out at the lake over which it could never fly
again.

Farther east, the road entered the Parque Nacional Vicente Pérez
Rosales in the shadow of Osorno. The vegetation became denser,
the turbulent Petrohué was glimpsed through the trees, and volcanic
mud slides obliterated portions of the dirt road, forcing detours.

The lodge is an old German farmhouse reputed to have hidden
the Nazi, Martin Bohrmann, during his flight from the vengeful Al-
lied victors. Now it is devoted to the innocent goal of housing and
feeding fly-fishing addicts. It would be the headquarters for our forays
into the Chilean wilderness in pursuit of lunker browns and rainbows.

The lodge, called Fundo el Salto—the Farm at the Falls—lies
just above Los Saltos (falls) de Petrohué. As we arrived we were immediately given a warm welcome. The staff is as *gemischt* as the population of Chile, not to speak of *los Estados Unidos*. A New Zealander,
Jan Williams, is the co-owner and hostess. René Yefi, a Mapuché
native Chilean, Marcelo Dufflocq, a Chilean of Basque origin, and
Gavin McPhail, an American, are the guides. And pisco sours, the
Chilean version of the Margarita, provided the universal international
glue that and every evening, not that they were really necessary for
that task.

The copper-skinned, stocky René was to be my guide. We developed an instant rapport. He is a man of few words, but expressive and
communicative nonetheless. To him I was *tranquilo*, as I later heard

from his colleagues. Between us we communicated by gesture and a word or two.

The countryside is reminiscent of the American Rockies, yet everything is somehow different. The granite peaks of the Andes, *la Cordillera*, are interspersed with snowcapped volcanic cones. The *Arrayan* tree, with its smooth bark, variegated white and brown, is a warmer version of the cold white and grey of the northern birch. The *Araucaria* pine, beautifully symmetrical and shapely, also called the Chile pine, or strangely enough, monkey-puzzle, is like no northern evergreen. It resembles instead some evergreens of New Zealand, which makes ecological sense, New Zealand being due west along the fortieth parallel albeit some 6000 miles distant. Nearly every bush, flower and tree is different. But I instantly recognized *la mora*, the introduced blackberry, which was everywhere, heavy with large, sweet berries. The greenness of the forest was accentuated by the bright red flowers of the wild fuchsia and the small, succulent red berries of the *murta* bush.

Well, what about the fishing? In this case I will not hesitate to say that, except for the Alaska trip, it was the greatest that I have ever enjoyed. A superlative indeed, since I have enjoyed all forays into new waters, finding pleasure in the surroundings regardless of the presence or absence of connections at the end of the fishing line.

All salmonids are newcomers to the Southern Hemisphere. The intrepid Scots and English coddled the fertilized ova on ice through the month–long voyages in the last century to remote outposts around the world. I believe there is now scarcely a year-round cold water stream in temperate surroundings that has not at one time been planted with trout. They have survived and flourished without further Man-assisted efforts of propagation in many southern waters of South America, New Zealand, and Tasmania.

René collected me early the next morning to initiate me to their secret motherlode of selective big trout. The trip from the lodge was a jolting jeep ride over barely recognizable tracks of recently cleared forest to the banks of the Rio Petrohué. The river was low and slightly off-color from melting snows following the late summer heat. It was a large river even now; judging from the extensive gravel and boulder banks, it can be a magnificent roaring torrent when in spate.

We embarked on one of the lodge's McKenzie dories downstream and across some rapids to the opposite shore; thence trudged inland to a verdant dale bisected by a meandering glassy-surfaced stream and flanked by floating banks of aquatic plants. The water was shockingly cold for that time of year—less than fifty degrees and clear as crystal. It was a true spring-fed creek, arising from an aquifer of the overhanging Sierra Santo Domingo range.

René's eagle, or should I say Indian, eyes, detected trout almost immediately, long before I could see them, when they had already detected me.

There was an occasional rise to unknown surface food. Accordingly, I adopted English chalkstream tactics, approached cautiously from downstream, and tried casting to the rises on my knees. The fly either landed on the opposite weed bank, usually impaling the vegetation, or it landed with a thud where a gently floating landing was essential. In either case the fish were put down. These wise lunkers would have none of it. Eventually I got the range and managed to prick a large trout on a small elkhair caddis. After that, surface activity ceased and we (rather René) changed tactics.

He tied on a dark olive wooly bugger with a good nine feet of leader terminating in size 4x. The instructions were to cast to the opposite bank and rapidly retrieve. This I did a few times until it happened. A dark shadow seemed to follow the fly. René pleaded, "Faster, faster!" Which I did and experienced the heart-stopping impact of a large fish grabbing the lure and heading off in a direction not consistent with my retrieve. The resultant forces produced the following reactions: the rod bent double, I stopped breathing, the hair-thin leader snapped. How many times, oh how many times has this befallen me? I assume that with experience comes wisdom and competence. Not necessarily so. However, this time it was not the fault of a carelessly tied–on leader or fly. No, because René had tied on all the tackle that day.

I sighed and went back to casting across the glassy surface into the weed bed. Eventually persistence was rewarded and a dark following shadow materialized into a full-bodied beautifully colored four-pound rainbow. How healthy and strong were these fish!

The rapid retrieve technique with the Wooly Bugger imitated the escape tactics of the *Pancora*, a small crustacean that resembles our Northern Hemisphere crawfish. The powerful backstroke with the tail often, but not always, saved the creature from a gastronomic end. Perhaps the long-ago transplanted browns and rainbows had genetically imprinted memories of this ancient and primitive prey.

The rest of the morning we spent in the single-minded quest for these elusive shadows. I was in a primal mode: no disturbing cerebration hindered the rhythm of the rod, the placement of the fly, or the confident reflex of the strike.

The sun was high and René called for a welcome halt to a memorable morning. We retreated to a shady grove and a sumptuous picnic was laid. Never have I enjoyed food and wine so much. The spicy Chilean salami appetizer was followed by a grilled chicken, freshly baked baguette, and crisp green salad, accompanied by good white and red wines. A long siesta followed. I dozed for an hour, then revived by stripping and plunging into a pool of the Petrohué. The bright sun warmed and dried me quickly. I thought of similar sensuous experiences such as on the Gairezi in Zimbabwe. Cold water, warm sun, a pure wilderness; are there more important things to experience?

The afternoon was devoted to a refinement of the morning's tactics. We devoted long periods to stalking a few fish. Slow wading through dense floating islands of weeds required René and me to steady each other with our arms on each other's shoulders. After painstakingly getting into range of the quarry, we could usually cast only once, netting and releasing a lunker trout if the cast was successful. If not, the fish and all his neighbors were put down for the duration. The intense concentration erased all sense of time. Suddenly it was dusk, time to make the rendezvous with Gavin and the pickup truck, and to return to an evening of good company, tall tales, pisco sours, and a late Hispanic supper.

The following day was spent in a grand float trip down ten miles of the majestic Petrohué. I began it shortly after dawn by wading just above a rapid and casting a dark olive wooly bugger across stream. At the third cast a vicious take woke me up. The fish was big and tough and I scrambled downstream to try to get below it, hoping for an upstream run against the tiring current. But no, it thought otherwise and slid downstream into the turbulent rapids. I was sure it was a goner as I scrambled, skipped, and stumbled downstream to try to keep up. Remarkably enough, the quarry decided to stop in a pool next to the bank, thus giving the resourceful René the opportunity to net it before it knew what was happening. It was a bright, well conditioned, five-pound brown, the only large brown that came to my net during that expedition. But a variety of rainbow and brook trout eventually compensated for that.

The rest of the day was devoted to floating down the magnificent river, down rapids, across glides, past deadfalls, through shallows and pools. I hooked and released dozens of fish but two events stand out clearly.

René was constantly at the oars, positioning me for the best casting position. At one deep pool he persisted in holding the boat in one spot just above an eddy. He urged me to cast again and again. Which I did, finally realizing the reason for his insistence. As the wooly bugger sank into the pool, there came not a rise, not a take; there came a convulsion, a subterranean eruption. The rod bent sharply, I had a truly big fish on, one that did not seem to mind the prick of the hook or the pull of the rod. René shouted, "Hola!" and pulled toward shore. I was too engaged with the muscle-wrenching task of dealing with the underwater leviathan to know what else was happening. The battle went on for countless minutes. Just as the underwater giant was near to revealing its shape and size there came the anticlimax. The line suddenly went limp, I retrieved the leader—and the fly, intact, except that the hook had snapped off. We gazed at it, open mouthed and dazed.

Why should a number four tempered steel hook break? Because, probably, no matter how carefully it is done, the act of pinching down the barb with pliers in order to facilitate the quick release of a fish will, as I have experienced before, weaken the hook.

René and I looked at each other, shook our heads, then smiled, and shook hands. It was a noble battle with a noble adversary—probably a fifteen-pound brown; but then, as we anglers all know, the one that gets away is always bigger than reality.

The other memorable skirmish happened as we floated past a deadfall. There was a swift current along the log. It looked like prime rainbow water, which was confirmed as the fly was grabbed on the surface in a mighty splash. The fish immediately dove into an underwater jungle of tree snags and I instinctively countered with precariously maximum side pressure. It desperately resisted and there was a seesaw battle in and around fallen trees and branches until I finally coaxed the fish out into open water. I continued the fight from the shore and finally beached and released it, a fine full-bodied, gorgeously colored rainbow of twenty-two inches.

We shared the picnic that day with the two other fishing parties in a wooded glen beside the river. A barbecue of lamb and sausages, accompanied by fresh vegetables and fruits, and Chilean wines, added a hedonistic dimension to the exhausting ardour of the chase. The siesta was a sweet anticlimax.

Early the next day, Manisha, René and Gavin, and I embarked in a small outboard-powered boat skippered by a local fisherman, Alejandro. The route was from Petrohué, the hamlet on the western shore of Lago Todos los Santos, straight across the large lake to the northeast shore where there was a landing jetty. There we picked up a trail into the national park, as Volcan Osorno's snow-capped cone glowed pink and orange from the light of the rising sun.

We hiked through alpine meadows and virgin forest to the upper reaches of the Rio la Junta, a small, rocky, mountain stream, that was a tributary of the larger Rio sin Nombre (River Without a Name). It was a fly-fishing heaven. Rainbows and brook trout to twelve inches rose to small dark terrestrials and pale-winged stoneflies. A three-weight rod and line sufficed for the delicate dry-fly presentations.

The morning's delicate techniques were balanced by brawnier methods in the afternoon, when we fished the mouth (*boca*) of the Rio sin Nombre on the sandy shore of the lake. Just as in Lake Taupo in New Zealand, big fish feed in the rip. Manisha and I hooked and released fat rainbows, one after another. I am sure night fishing, as in Taupo, would have resulted in much larger fish including browns that lurk in the depths of the lake.

The end of a perfect fishing day turned into a wet, chilling slog back across the lake to Petrohué. Perhaps the Fishgod was annoyed at the exceptional experience despite the fact that none of his minions had been seriously harmed during all these days. The wind blew east across Lago Todos los Santos and the small boat slammed into breaking waves every other second, with cold spume smarting in our faces. The pisco sours that evening were doubly welcome.

We explored the outlet of the lake into the Rio Petrohué early next morning. Alongside one bank was an eddy produced by a downstream cliff. The bank was ringed by shrubs that held hundreds of small, cream colored stoneflies, some of which fluttered and touched down on the river surface. There was constant subsurface activity at the tail end of the eddy. I tied on a variety of small, pale, dry flies, all of which were rejected. René and I watched, speculated, and experimented. René said, " They are taking emergers!" He tied on a pale pupa imitation and I let it float down into the hotbed of activity. There was a swirl and I reflexively struck. The flyless leader came back into my face. Oh Lord, give me the patience but also the wisdom to be a good fisherman! A 3x tippet for five-pound trout is not the same as a 6x tippet for one-pounders.

The week was over. The lessons were learned—again. I departed from Fundo el Salto a happy man. My wife had come to understand a bit more about the magnificent obsession of angling, a very gentle sport, harmless really, in the midst of this rather violent world.

The next year I explored farther south in Chilean Patagonia.

Coyhaique is the capitol of *Region XI* of Chile, which has twelve such districts extending in order from North to South. The plane was nearly empty in the first leg of the flight from Santiago to Coyhaique. In Puerto Montt it filled to capacity, reminiscent of many bus rides I experienced in India, with huge amounts of baggage, cartons, babies, and solemn, handsome Mapuchés. Everything short of crates of squawking chickens piled on board.

I could see why. The topography changed dramatically after Puerto Montt. The verdant landscape, dotted with neat Germanic homesteads around Puerto Montt, gave place to a wilderness of rocky islands and fjords flanked by steep cliffs and plateaus. Snow fields nestled between jagged peaks. Surely this was Norway.

Coyhaique appeared: massive buttes of basalt overhung a frontier town. Rain squalls drove down on a landscape that reminded me of Montana. Nearly all the traffic consisted of four-wheel drive utility vehicles. My lodging, just outside the dusty town, was on the banks of the Rio Simpson. My guide was Alex Prior, a pleasant, competent-appearing Uraguayan in his thirties. By previous arrangement I was to be on my own for the first week, the idea of being guided still clashing with my instinct for independent exploration. But I surely needed him on the ultimate trip to the Rio Baker.

It was eight in the evening and dusk was settling over the rugged valley. Mayflies were everywhere. The roar of the rapids stirred predatory piscatory instincts. I rapidly mounted the rod and walked down to the river. The deep pool seemed to be a volcanic cauldron, with bubbles everywhere.

But no, they were the rises of trout to the evening hatch. The first cast landed a fat and healthy Chilean rainbow, and so did the second and third casts. I placed the fourth cast far out in the center of the pool and an enthusiastic response broke off the fly. The freed fish thumped his tail at me with a formidable splash. By this time it was too dark to tie on a new fly, and I returned to my cabin with the warm glow of, for once, a successful start on a fishing trip.

The next morning I decided to give fishing a rest and explore a bit of Chile. From the right bank of Rio Simpson, rising toward massive basalt buttes was one of the many nature preserves extending along the the western Andean slope. The morning was cold but the sun, bright. The dirt road ascended several thousand feet through several ecoclimes. There was first the deforested *pampa* and a few scattered small landholdings, each with wind-sheltered and fenced plots of potatoes, carrots, and cabbage. The road steepened as I entered a sparse forest. The small pines with long bare trunks (*Pinus contorta*) and wild fuchsias with brilliant red blossoms gradually gave way to a lush forest of tall trees and dense ground covers of ivy. Thick clumps of Patagonian bamboo (*Chusgura colea*), smaller than the asiatic variety, were gradually displaced by increasingly dense evergreen forest. The gloom of the forest floor reminded me of the troll forests of Scandinavia. But I saw no fleeting figures here. Possibly the Southern Hemisphere was spared these mischievous elves that are related to Leprechauns and other northern semihominids.

I walked past a chain of small lakes, barely visible through the dense foliage. What a blessing, for I was hot and sweaty from the climb. I walked down to a pond, stripped, and immersed into the limpid coolness. Ducks moved away to give me room. The sun peeked through the stands of giant southern beeches (*Lenga*), of which only few remain following the indiscriminate timbering of decades ago. The chill of my wet body was only partly relieved by the warmth of the elusive sun. It was time to move on. The downhill walk took less time, enough for an evening of fishing on the Simpson.

At eight thirty, the sun was setting and darkness descended on the brawling stream. Several hatches—one of golden grey mayflies, another of pale Caddis—erupted over the river surface. It began with a few rises dimpling the water. Soon the Caddis were fluttering everywhere, landing on my face, nearly inhaled with each breath. The dimples moved to a boil and nearly each cast connected with madly feeding rainbows ranging from six to fifteen inches. Then, suddenly, twenty minutes after the hatch started, all activity stopped. It was quite dark by then. I could barely see enough to retrace my steps up the steep bank and back to the lodge and the anticipation of pisco sours, a roaring fire, and pleasant company.

And so it went for nearly a week. I hired a four-wheel-drive pickup and explored further stretches of the Simpson and several lakes. The countryside was beautifully wild with an ever changing landscape of mountains, hills, meadows, woods, streams and lakes. Weatherfronts from the Pacific boiled up dramatically over the western peaks and bore down on me with violent but brief squalls. Peaceful siestas after a picnic lunch, always with a new Chilean wine, writing, and reading—this was the life!

But the relaxed, indulgent period came to an end. The next was serious business: the planned foray south to the Rio Baker, largest of all rivers draining into the south Pacific.

Alex picked me up in his jeep one morning and we embarked. The dirt track given the exalted name of Camino Austral is the latest en-

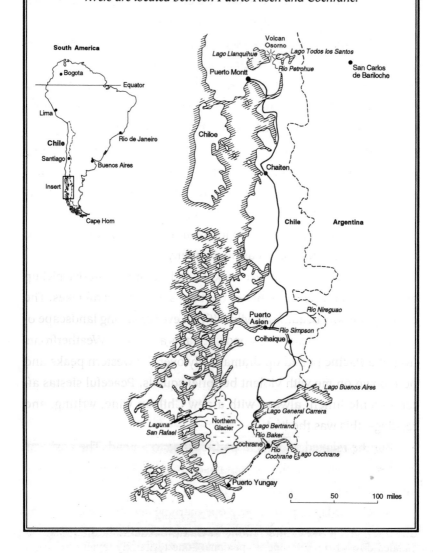

ROUTE OF CAMINO AUSTRAL FROM PUERTO MONTT
AT THE SOUTHERN END OF THE CHILEAN LAKE DISTRICT TO
PUERTO YUNGAY IN THE HEART OF WESTERN PATAGONIA.

*Rio Petrohué lies east of Puerto Montt. The other described
rivers are located between Puerto Aisen and Cochrane.*

gineering achievement of Chile in extending its road system ultimately from one end to the other of the country's 3000-mile length. But it ends now at Puerto Yungay, just south of our destination, the town of Cochran, named after the nineteenth-century English lord and freebooter who helped to build the Chilean navy.

Although it was February, the antipodal summer, we ran into snow squalls at 5000 feet, a few hours south of Coyhaique. The road then led for miles through a desolated landscape of ash and dead trees, the fringe of fallout from the gigantic Volcan Hudson eruption of 1985. We descended a steep ridge and saw a range of snow-clad peaks stretching southward to the west. The first, Cerro Castillo, truly resembled a castle; a dozen spires thrust upward from the snow and glaciers mantling the base of this dramatic mountain. It was a mountaineer's dream, or, perhaps, nightmare.

Driving along the dusty road, we saw to the west large rivers, ranging in color from opal green to mud brown, emerging from the crevasses of canyons stretching up into a vast ice field, *el Campo de Hielo Norte*. I located this immense glacier on a topographic map in Hans Steffen's monumental *Westpatagonien*, printed 1915—in German (although Steffen was Chilean and a professor at the University of Santiago).

By evening we had reached the shore of the immense Lago General Carrera which extended to the west into Argentina, where it was called Lago Buenos Aires. The Chileans and Argentinians seem not to agree on many things. Dramatic cloud formations erupted over the glacier field as dusk approached and bore down on us with startling speed. Rain, snow, hail, wind, and sun all took turns in a meteorological symphony. The single outlet of the lake was the source of the Rio Baker. The first stage, however, is the long, narrow Lago Bertrand which we reached as night fell.

This was the welcome overnight stop at the lodge of Orlando Scarito Küpfer, an affable and energetic young Chilean of German and Italian origin. He had, nearly single-handedly, built a lovely guest lodge with a variety of beautifully finished local woods. The view from the porch at sunset was spectacular. The dark blue of the lake contrasted with the dazzling white of the snow fields at the base of pinnacles starkly silhouetted by constantly changing cloud formations of unusual and dramatic cumulo-cirrhus patterns. The clouds reflected a progressive spectrum of color and shade from flamboyant oranges and pinks, ending in dignified deep purple hues.

Orlando was also flamboyant, but in a proper Iberian culture, dignified. We shared an unforgettable evening of conversation, his Spanish, Alex's linguistic mediation, and my English. The early history of Patagonia recalled that of the American West. Orlando's father came down as a young man into the timber trade in Patagonia. It was, appropriately, also the refuge of Butch Cassidy and the Sundance Kid. The land was limitless and the sky, day and night, spectacular. I could sense the love of this virgin landscape that Orlando cherished. But logging interests were on the move, the Japanese were hungry for timber. I had already seen some of the beginning devastation. With this newly completed road to the south there would be an escalation of exploitation.

The next morning we fished the headwaters of Rio Baker, below the outlet of Lago Bertrand. The power of this river was overwhelming: huge rapids created a pounding din in my ears. Alex stationed me just to the side of the main current in a large eddy. The cold, clear water even here tore at my waders as I cast large wooly buggers close to the surging waves. The fishing was slow and hard, the season was late, but I connected with enough heavy rainbows to tire my arms and quell my predatory instincts. The largest was probably six pounds. Alex was disappointed and directed me to new spots but I was satisfied and looked forward to the streamside lunch: Chilean wine, sausage, cheese, and bread followed by fruit was my idea of heaven. This pattern repeated the following day before we drove the final leg down to Cochrane, a total distance of 240 miles from Coyhaique, all on a two-lane dirt road.

The Rio Cochrane is to the Baker as the moon is to the sun. A gentle tributary, its beauty is in the marvellous clarity yet beautiful hues of green and blue in deep pools, and the great variety of rapids, riffles, glides, and flats.

Tomassin, quiet, strong, a superb boatman, brought us upriver in his large boat that was used for transporting bales of wool down from the estancias around Lago Cochrane.

The wooden craft pushed across a bight of the river, Lago Chico, then entered a narrow, tortuous canyon where the river assumed all the virtues of great trout water, pools, rapids, riffles, runs, and falls. Tomassin miraculously guided the boat up the main channel, avoiding by inches jutting boulders and deadfall.

We landed on a small peninsula and set up camp. The fishing was like that in New Zealand, by sight, because the fish were few but big. So I watched and waited until, in the middle of a run before a rapid, I saw a subtle rise, not a feisty, juvenile splash but a dimple that signaled a big trout, like the one I fondly recalled from the Tainionvirta in Finland. It refused the repeated drift of an elkhair caddis, and I resorted to a streamer that I dragged across stream to finally connect with a vigorous rainbow. But further searching for big trout in big pools that day was fruitless. The pools had confusing and contrary currents that dragged my bugger willynilly and scarcely fooled the huge and wise old browns that Tomassin, but not I, saw on the bottom.

We enjoyed a huge Chilean picnic. A two-hour siesta followed and I alternatively dozed and read the *Red Badge of Courage* for the second or third time. I spent some more hours of fly-fishing in, for me, the most lovely little river since the Gairezi. Presently we broke camp and returned downstream. In the lake we trolled, somewhat shamefacedly as fly fishermen but landed beautifully colored, powerful browns along the way.

The magic moment came at dusk. We beached the boat at the outlet of the lake and searched for rises. The tail was a long and wide glide and riffle. The light was failing. The caddis hatch was sporadic but soon some subtle but promising rises appeared, the widening rings on the mirrored surface reflecting the orange sunset. I had waded out nearly up to my armpits and the distance was still extreme, for me. But, for once in Patagonia, the wind had died and with judicious and lucky casting I reached the rises some sixty feet away. Two nips were followed by a solid take—a splash and flurry signalled through the fly-line a substantial weight. The distant acrobatics were spectacular; even Tomassin was impressed. The fish ran and the reel screamed. Then it turned, aggressively, towards me and I frantically retrieved line hand over hand, desperately trying to take up slack. Finally, in the darkness, it tired and I was able to retrieve the large fish for the obligatory photograph before the eventual release of a beautifully conditioned six-pound rainbow.

I thought that there was little more to amaze me in this wonderful land. I did not count, however, in what follows, on being the first to recognize and describe a new species of trout.

Alex and I returned to Coyhaique tired and happy. He handed me over to a colleague, the Montanan Mike Mozolf, who led me to the Rio Nireguao some seventy kilometers north of Coyhaique. We drove through a semiarid landscape that was, appropriately, reminiscent of Montana. The stream is a placid meandering small river, flanked by lush grassy prairie. The principal, if not only prey, of trout in this stream is the grasshopper.

And so it was that Dave's Hopper was all that we needed all day to lure a variety of browns of up to four pounds. It was great fun, but the most startling experience was to see, with eyewitness confirmation, a two-foot brown leap totally out of the water, onto the opposite bank, obviously after an oblivious grasshopper innocently sunning itself. The trout remained on the bank a few seconds before it slithered back into the water. The scene reminded me of video films from the Patagonian coast of killer whales beaching themselves when chasing seals sunning themselves on the shore. I took the opportunity to give a name to the Nireguao browns—"*Salmo trutta var. Montanus ascendere.*" Translation, mountain-climbing trout. I hope that the International Commission on Zoological Nomenclature will consider my recommendation.

The Ancient Angler

T HE DEERFIELD WAS RUNNING HIGH AND COLD, but the air was warm and dry. It was April. The occasional mayfly dipped down to the water's surface, the skunkweed pushed up shoots, but there were no blackflies to be seen or felt. No, because my thermometer registered a water temperature of thirty-eight degrees. Blackflies hatch at forty-four degrees.

I saw him downstream, a thin, bent figure, wading in water up to his thighs, flicking the flyline out into the deep swirl just below the rapids. He wore a new fore-and-aft deerstalker-style fishing hat, but the tattered and mended vest and waders looked as old as he. On closer look the rod was vintage fiberglass and the reel was an ageless Pflueger.

The incongruous hat must have been a birthday or Christmas present.

I began fishing a respectable distance above until he retreated to a rock to change flies. Moving past, I commented, " The water is really cold—thirty-eight degrees."

He looked up and said, "I'm not surprised. Only fishing nuts like us go out this early. Any hits?"

"None."

"What are you using?"

"An olive Wooly Bugger," I answered.

"I tried a Mickey Finn fished deep, but no luck."

I saw the newly tied-on Hare's Ear nymph a foot behind a one-eighth ounce sinker. He was fishing *really* deep. I cast a nymph into the glide below the pool, feeling the pleasant contrast of the warm sun on my upper half and cold seeping through my waders on the lower. The roar of the rapids echoed between the walls of the narrow canyon, drowning the calls of the chickadees and titmice, and even the jays.

The old man stopped to change flies again. I moved up and asked, "Have you fished here before? Is it a good spot?"

"You bet it is. There're always good fish here. This your first time?"

"Yes, I'm exploring from here up to Vermont today."

He peered closely at me through watery eyes. I apparently passed muster as a fellow fly-fisherman, for he proceeded to give me a thorough description of this, the catch-and-release section of the Massachusetts Deerfield. I was cautioned about the sudden rise of river levels following release of water upstream at the power station, and about the bus-loads of kayakers that descended on the river like locusts, on weekends.

"I don't mind their having fun but they sure clutter up the river and put the fish down."

As we chatted I noted his fishing license in a glassine case pinned to the vest. The birthdate was 1907 and the name was old New England Yankee. His age would be eighty-seven. That number reminded me of something. "Fourscore and seven years ago. . . ." Lincoln harkened back to the Declaration of Independence. Just twice this old man's lifespan would reach back to that milestone of history. How close he was to great men and great events. I felt through those pale blue eyes a direct connection with that past.

We tarried longer, exchanging fishing tales, knowing that there would be no hits this day.

"You'll find a good hole on the West River, just at the mouth of Houghton Brook. Drive through South Londonderry, past the campground, swing down to the river and hike downstream. Nobody else knows about it except, maybe, the locals. The're some big square-tails in there."

The parchment-thin skin crinkled as he smiled, recalling past pleasures. Would I, too, fish this cold river if I reached his age? Would I, too, be at peace with the Fishgod? We returned to our fishing but there was no sign of action that day.

Presently he gave a wave of farewell and waded back to the shore. I moved up to his more favorable spot but watched as he clambered up the steep hillside.

The old man, encumbered with rod and wading staff, made painfully slow progress up the nearly vertical slope. He pushed his rod ahead, grasped projecting rocks and roots, and cautiously inched himself up. I watched anxiously, debating whether or not to go to his aid. No, I was sure that he would refuse.

Finally, he reached the top, sat down to rest, and gave me a wave to say, "All is well."

I blinked in the strong sunlight and he was gone.

Index

private place, 58-9, 62-3

Q
quail, 18

R
rituals, Scandinavian, 8-9
Rod in India, The, 108

S
salmon, 141-2; diminished
   supply, 96; fishery in Norway,
   121-3; kelts, 27; spawning,
   29
sauna, 14, 124
Scandinavia, fly fishing in,
   119-29; ritual, 6-11
sea trout, 121
seasons, effect on fishing, 25-7
secret memories, 57
shad, edibility of, 98-9; as
   fishing challenge, 95-101;
   history of, 96, 101; "poor
   man's salmon," 5
silver salmon, 18-19
smörgåsbord, 124
Spain, fishing expedition in,
   41-2
Sri Lanka, animal life, 69;
   colonial accommodations,
   67-8, 70-71; fishing expedition in, 65, 68-71

steelhead, 7
surströmming. See herring.
Sweden, fishing for cod, 52;
   hospitality in, 124
Switzerland, fly fishing in,
   143

T
tea, in Turkey, 36
tea plantation, working in, 66
Thomas, Henry S, writing about
   fishing, 108
toddy, culture of, 66-7
Towers of Trebizond, The, 35
trolling, 161
trout, brookies, 21, 22; brown,
   21-22, 29-30, 37, 59-61,
   62, 70-1, 85, 122; in
   California, 17, 18; catch-and-
   release, 30; Central Asia,
   40-1; and green oak caterpillars, 24-5; in Finland, 127-9;
   lunkers, 22, 29-30; New
   Zealand, 90-1, 92-3; in
   Patagonia, 149-53; rainbow,
   39, 69-70, 77, 78, 79-80, 134,
   143; 154-5, 156-7, 160-1,
   162-3; Swiss brownies, 46-8,
   49
turbot. See cod.
Turkey, fishing expedition in,
   34-37

1

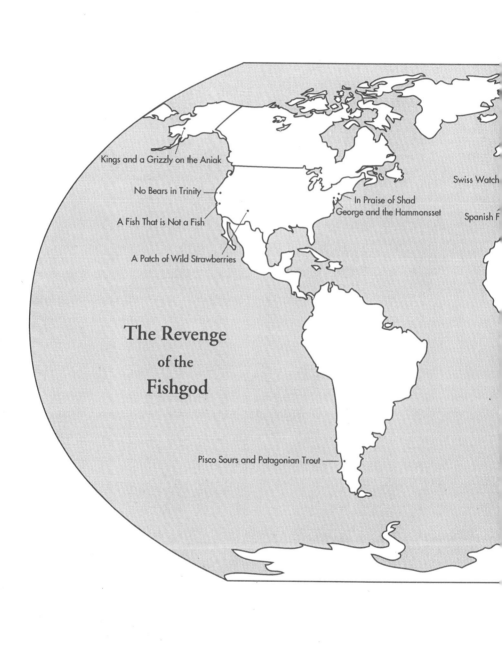

Kings and a Grizzly on the Aniak

No Bears in Trinity

A Fish That is Not a Fish

A Patch of Wild Strawberries

Swiss Watch

In Praise of Shad
George and the Hammonsset

Spanish F

The Revenge
of the
Fishgod

Pisco Sours and Patagonian Trout